It is the great irony of our day that, in a world where more and more people *know* that the future will look very different from the past, the most visible stories of the present seem more and more driven by desperate, fear-driven efforts to return to the past. In a time when it is easy to set aside hope as naïve, Michele Hunt reminds us that all change starts with protecting that small spark of possibility and then takes us on a tour of amazing fire protectors around the world.
Peter Senge, MIT and Academy for System Change

Michele Hunt is the ultimate DreamMaker. Her inspiring book is a "beacon of hope" for all of us. Her stories give us great comfort that there are remarkable people among us who are leaving "no stone unturned" and meeting whatever challenges they face to make this a better world for all of us.
Joseph M. Brodecki, Principal, Bernstein Global Wealth Management; Presidential (of the United States) appointee to the United States Holocaust Memorial Museum Council

How Michele Hunt can find so many wonderful innovations for the common good, I don't know. Her book about the people who are changing things for the better will uplift your spirit.
Max De Pree, Former Chairman and CEO of Herman Miller, Inc.; author of *Leadership is an Art*

Another amazing book by an amazing author, which is a must-read for all that are concerned about the future, and the future of our society and the future of our children. Michele Hunt has carefully crafted stories of leaders, of dreams and of business realities that can serve as a benchmark to others. If you care, if you want to be touched and join the dreamers in action, read this book.
Simon L. Dolan, Professor, ESADE Future of Work Chair & President of the Board of Trustees – Global Future of Work Foundation

DreamMakers not only inspires you to realize the greater good that only you can do, but shows how to get it done. The powerful individuals, stories, and insights Michele Hunt shares will change your life for the better so that you can do the same for others.
Simon Mainwaring, CEO, We First, and author of *New York Times* **bestseller** *We First*

For anyone who's felt the call to work in a way that's less about the balance sheet and more about balance in the world, Michele Hunt offers a much-needed infusion of optimism and inspiration. This collection of wisdom from those who are redefining corporate sustainability and social good will kindle the human spirit in the work we do.
Lyell Clarke, President and CEO, Clarke

Michele shares the journeys of leaders, entrepreneurs, and communities who fearlessly dream a positive future for humankind and the planet. These inspiring people have committed their lives in service to making that beautiful dream come true. This book is about hope. It invites us all to look inside our hearts and discover our unique spirit of DreamMaking, and put that force to work to help create a flourishing world.

Frances Hesselbein, President and CEO of The Frances Hesselbein Leadership Institute; Editor-in-Chief of *Leader to Leader* Journal; US Presidential Medal of Freedom

This extraordinary narrative of doing well by doing good, brought to life through intimate stories and the author's incisive commentary, reminds us of the possibility that we each have to create a desired future – one in which people thrive, businesses prosper, and the planet flourishes. Through this book you will meet the people next door who are changing the world for the better, many of them in the face of great adversity. Michele Hunt writes with the insight and pragmatism gained from a life well lived.

Chris Laszlo, Chair and Chuck Fowler Professor of Business as an Agent of World Benefit, Department of Organizational Behavior, The Weatherhead School of Management; Faculty Executive Director, The Fowler Center, Case Western Reserve University

In *DreamMakers,* Michele shines a light on stories of innovation that are helping to write a new and positive narrative for humanity. These stories are not only inspirational, however, they are also invitational. They invite each of us to shine a light on our own passions and talents to help create a flourishing world in our unique spheres of influence. From envisioning our families, to our organizations, to our entire communities as catalysts for the greater good, Michele reminds us that we can all be DreamMakers!

Lindsey Godwin, Professor and Director of the Cooperrider Center for Appreciative Inquiry, Champlain College

What an inspiration to read Michele Hunt's new book! Sharing with us the inspiration and lessons learned from incredible individuals who relentlessly and successfully have acted upon their vision for a better world, Michele Hunt gives us hope. May reading this book become the defining moment for us all, helping us awaken our own DreamMaker. We can – and should – all take part in the quiet revolution to build a brand new world where people, planet, and business all prosper. Showing the way, this book is just what the world needs in these troubled times.

Inrgid Stange, Founder and Chair, Partnership for Change, Oslo, Norway

DreamMakers

Innovating for the Greater Good

Michele Hunt

DreamMakers

Innovating for the **Greater Good**

Greenleaf
PUBLISHING

© 2017 Greenleaf Publishing

Published by Greenleaf Publishing Limited
Salts Mill, Victoria Road, Saltaire, BD18 3LA, UK
www.greenleaf-publishing.com

Cover by Sadie Gornall-Jones

Printed and bound by Printondemand-worldwide.com, UK

British Library Cataloguing in Publication Data:
    A catalogue record for this book is available from the British Library.

    ISBN-13: 978-1-78353-568-2 [paperback]
    ISBN-13: 978-1-78353-395-4 [hardback]
    ISBN-13: 978-1-78353-567-5 [PDF ebook]
    ISBN-13: 978-1-78353-569-9 [ePub ebook]

This book is dedicated to my father, Theodore Hunt, Sr., the greatest man I have ever met. His boundless love, his endless generosity and his tireless pursuit of creating a world where everyone is valued, heard, and respected, defined him. He helped to uplift the lives of thousands. He taught people, especially young people, to believe in the mantra *I Am Somebody*. Most precious to my heart, Dad taught me to be a DreamMaker.

And to my mother, Leona Hunt, thank you for *always* being there for me. You are a gentle lady who has the wisdom of a sage, the inner strength of a warrior and the gentle heart of a goddess. You are the most beautiful person I have ever known.

And to my daughter, Nicole Levey Hunt, thank you for being my greatest cheerleader. You were relentless at keeping me going when I got weary, and, when doubt reared its ugly head, your love, words, and your support helped me to find my footing. I deeply respect you for living your values. You had the courage to walk away from a lucrative job on Wall Street to help elect and support a great leader, President Barack Obama, during two campaigns. You are one of the brightest people I know and the brightest light in my life.

Contents

Part 2
Blurring the lines

Part 3
We The People

Foreword

Roberta Baskin

Michele Hunt shows us how to dream BIG for the greater good. She has spent her life honing her DreamMaker skills and catalyzing leaders to explore their own paths towards creating a better world. Here, Michele takes us on a quest to discover extraordinary DreamMakers. As she illustrates throughout, it is "business" that has the imaginative spark, the resources, and business acumen to develop a brighter future for humanity, especially when they collaborate with organizations and communities around the world. Michele's thoughtful interviews reveal what it takes to tackle major obstacles and become a successful entrepreneur through perseverance and empowerment.

We're living in times of extraordinary disruption and uncertainty. Michele shows us why *now* is exactly the right time for business leaders to step up. Our elected politicians are caught in gridlock causing public despair and distrust. But Michele amplifies hope: the kind of hope we rarely see or hear in our daily news reports. Over the course of 20 years, Michele has discovered there is much to celebrate thanks to an emerging breed of business leader. In the wake of the disarray caused by global political leadership, business leaders are stepping up, writing new rules for business conduct. Using the tools of technology, common sense, and collaboration, business leaders are addressing many of the world's thorniest challenges.

Michele's research reveals the architecture of a positive, dynamic global movement. She amplifies stories of courageous leadership that serve as motivating examples of what humanity is capable of and *who* we can become. The shift has already begun. In September 2015 the United Nations voted unanimously to approve a global "To Do" list to achieve by 2030. The UN's 17 Sustainable Development Goals, which Michele showcases in her preface, could be worth trillions of dollars in opportunities for business leaders who produce innovative solutions.

The choices we make about how we live, what we produce, what we buy, and how we live can destroy or transform life on our planet. It will take DreamMakers to boldly confront and conquer climate change, the refugee crisis, feeding the hungry, and stopping terrorism. The DreamMakers among us will help us shift to a world of renewable energy, unlimited food and education, and peace and prosperity for all.

In DreamMakers, Michele introduces us to a group of modern-day explorers charting the course toward global transformation. They create bold visions, then turn them into reality. Michele shows how authentic leadership creates community, collaboration, and celebration. All of the businesses she profiles create a culture of caring and empathy. Employees consider themselves as family, friends, and kindred spirits. There's genuine pride in the work they do; a shared purpose beyond profit.

And these heroes in business are never complacent. They are life-long learners, like Michele herself. At the end of each chapter there is a passage of self-discovery where Michele reflects on what she has learned from the personal story of each inspiring DreamMaker. Michele's wisdom and enthusiasm are imbedded in every DreamMaker interview she conducts. She circled the globe collecting unique insights from business leaders who fulfilled their dreams. Some of these leaders, such as businessman, philanthropist, and educator Chuck Fowler have been spinning their magic for decades. Others, like the Junior Enterprisers, are emboldened by their early successes and setting the bar higher to achieve more.

The result is a blueprint of practical ways to think and behave as a leader.

When you finish *DreamMakers*, you will see just how interconnected we all are, and how vital it is to co-create a new story for a better world. *DreamMakers* inspires hope and reveals opportunities for creating the world we all want; solutions that respect humanity and nurture Mother Nature.

Roberta Baskin, Executive Director of AIM2Flourish, is an award-winning investigative journalist, with Peabody, DuPont–Columbia, and multiple Emmy awards to her name. She is the former senior Washington correspondent for *NOW with Bill Moyers*, senior investigative producer for the ABC News magazine *20/20*, chief investigative correspondent for the CBS News magazine *48 Hours*, and has contributed special reports to the *CBS Evening News*.

Preface

I believe we can change the world. My passion is seeking out and shining a light on people, businesses and organizations, and communities that are doing just that. I call these people **DreamMakers**. These inspiring people have found the courage to dream big and are taking on seemingly intractable problems such as war, poverty, the degradation of the planet, global health, illiteracy, hate, and prejudice. They see the world, and everyone and everything around it, as an interconnected, interdependent living organism. DreamMakers understand that human beings are capable of rethinking, redesigning, and co-creating a brand new world. They are birthing an evolved world-view; **doing well by doing good** is becoming the new definition of success for the 21st century. They are proving that by innovating for the greater good we can accomplish both our personal goals *and* together co-create a world where people and the planet can flourish.

I went on this journey to engage DreamMakers because I felt a sense of frustration, anxiety, and even fear, which many of us are experiencing in these turbulent times. People everywhere are searching for examples of new ways of living, leading, working, and being in our evolving world. My mission is to share these "pockets of hope" wherever and however I can, to inspire people around the world to find the courage to come together and transform our troubled world into a planet where well-being and flourishing defines us.

On my 20-year quest to discover what we can learn from DreamMakers, I noticed common qualities in their character, behavior and decision-making. I wanted to know if they shared a common perspective, values, and consciousness. I discovered that indeed they did. As I interviewed people for my books, articles, and documentary, it seemed I was always talking to the same person. They all share attitudes and beliefs that transcend who they are, where they live, or their individual circumstances. They lead their lives with a compelling positive vision that is born out of their deeply held belief that people and the planet are sacred. They have the wisdom to align with others who share their vision and values, and the confidence and self-discipline to commit to making their dreams come true. In short, DreamMakers are optimistic, passionate, creative people committed to changing the world. I discovered nine characteristics DreamMakers have in common:[1]

DreamMakers shared characteristics

1. **How they see the world.** DreamMakers share a sense of responsibility beyond their own lives. They take responsibility for the world they live in and are committed to making it better. They share a characteristic I call "practical optimism"; although they clearly perceive current reality, they unflinchingly confront it. They have a deep belief that any challenge can be overcome. Their visions are large, deep, and unaffected by cynicism, and their values are rooted in love and transcend all boundaries.

2. **How they treat people and nature.** DreamMakers have a deep faith in people, in their capabilities, potential, and basic goodness. Interpersonal relationships are precious to

---

[1]   I have written about the shared characteristics of DreamMakers in my book Hunt, M. (1998) *DreamMakers: Putting Vision and Values to Work*. Mountain View, CA: Davies Black, and in my blog at www.huffingtonpost. com.

them and at the heart of everything they do. They see the environment and the planet as our life-support system and treat them with the love and respect they deserve. They understand that we are inextricably connected to everyone and everything, and therefore lead their lives, businesses, organizations, and communities with a reverence for all human relationships and the planet that supports us.

3. **How they make decisions.** DreamMakers feel deeply about things; they are deliberate and conscientious. They consider the benefits and the consequences of their actions. They trust their intuition *and* consider the knowledge and judgment of others. They make decisions with their head and their heart; however, when their logic and their feelings are at odds they always go with their heart.

4. **How they build teams.** DreamMakers focus on people's strengths. They understand that we are all flawed, so they build teams that fill our weak spots, allowing us to focus on our strengths and others to complement us with their strengths. They have experienced the power of collaboration and cooperation in accomplishing goals, achieving superior results, and celebrating shared success. They know that we can accomplish much more together than any one of us can accomplish alone. They also feel a deep, transcending basic human desire for a sense of belonging and community.

5. **How they use creativity.** DreamMakers allow creativity to soar. They share a spirit of invention, believing that any breakthrough idea or product requires an environment that fosters freedom, diverse perspectives, experimentation, risk, and play.

6. **How they act.** DreamMakers are out of step with the norm—ahead of their time. They succeed not because they lead us to reconcile ourselves with the current reality but because they help us see that we can change it.

7. **How they respond to fear and "failure."** *DreamMakers* stay focused on their purpose, vision, and values. When feelings of insecurity and anxiety surface, and they always do, they lift their minds to their higher purpose and their compelling vision. They use their values to remind them of what is truly important in life. They are courageous and resilient. They have all faced tremendous challenges, made mistakes, and "failed" multiple times. They also learn from their "failures" and bounce back quicker, stronger, and wiser.

8. **How they learn and grow.** DreamMakers have an insatiable appetite for new information and different perspectives. They look to everyone and every situation to learn and grow. They are multi-dimensional—deeply involved in and with their family, their community, the arts, and the environment, as well as their work. They derive their knowledge and wisdom from all these sources, which gives them a rich array of ideas and choices.

9. **How they are anchored.** DreamMakers believe they are a part of something much greater and grander than themselves. Some call it "God," some call it an "invisible wholeness," and others refer to it as a "field of energy." Regardless of what they call it, they sense the deep connection between everyone and everything. They feel deeply connected to a higher purpose and a higher power, and they see their lives and their work as an expression of divine spirit.

It has probably become apparent that I am an unapologetic optimist. My optimism does not come from idealistic notions of Utopia or Pollyannaish sensibilities; it comes from my life experiences. My life journey has given me a glimpse of what is possible. My childhood, my education, my professional experiences, and the people I have met while on my journey creating my books, blogs, articles, and documentary have taught me a great deal about **DreamMaking**.

I was born into the lives of two beautiful, remarkable DreamMakers, Ted and Leona Hunt. My parents led our family with a compelling positive vision for ourselves, born out of the values that mattered to them most. They came from challenging beginnings. Dad was the second oldest of 12 children in a family that had tremendous financial challenges. My mother was the oldest of four and lost her mom when she was seven—her father left so the kids were moved around from family to family. At the age of eight my mother effectively became her siblings' mother and protector. When my parents married they made a conscious decision to co-create a vision of the family they wanted to create together, and the values they wanted to guide their decisions and behavior. At a time when being a Black in America was tremendously challenging, especially in our life circumstances, they helped us to see that it is possible to make our personal hopes and dreams come true by doing good in the world. They helped us to understand that any obstacle can be overcome. They also taught us that all people and all living things deserve our love, compassion, and support.

My parents' vision and values helped us to navigate through some tremendous obstacles.[2] While I was growing up my father's job was to help bring racial harmony to military bases. As a result, we were frequently one of the first Black families to live on base. My early years of school were in places that were not hospitable to Blacks. The elementary school environment in the South in the late 1950s provided a particularly tough testing ground for my brothers and me. My family experienced all of the intended and unintended humiliations Black Americans in the South had to endure: separate drinking fountains, prohibited from using public restrooms, and barred from eating in restaurants. Because we were often the only black families on base, we also experienced some very tough personal challenges. Living in Fort Campbell, Kentucky, we were called the "N-word" 30, 40 times a day—and not just by the children. When we went out to play the children would lock their arms and sing "tick tock the game is locked no niggers can play"; it was a ritual.

---

[2] I have told some of my story in Hunt, M. (2011, April 1) My story: An exciting and challenging childhood. [Blogpost]. Retrieved from http://michelehunt.blogspot.co.uk/2011/04/my-story-exciting-and-challenging.html.

But my parents prepared us to navigate through those tough times. Every morning before I left for school my father would make me stand before the bathroom mirror, look at myself, and repeat seven times "I am healthy, happy, beautiful, intelligent, loving, loved, and wise." I remember thinking to myself, "and you are crazy." When I came home from school after encountering many challenges, I would complain to my mother. My mother holds deeply the value of personal responsibility. She would listen patiently but she would always respond by saying "yes baby, okay sweetheart—now what are you going to do about it?" So between my father giving me a positive personal vision of myself, and my mother teaching me the value of personal responsibility, I learned a powerful lesson: by living with a sense of purpose, a compelling vision and deeply held values, we can make our dreams come true against tremendous obstacles, *and* help to create a better world for ourselves and others.

In my twenties I found DreamMakers in a very unlikely place—a state prison for adult male felons in the Michigan Department of Corrections. While serving as Deputy Warden of Programs for Rehabilitation, I discovered that when the inmates were given the opportunity to authentically participate in the design of programs that affected them, they transformed into DreamMakers. In collaboration with the treatment staff, the prison guards, and the community volunteers, they co-created remarkably effective programs that helped to equip the men with the skills and the values to live productive lives in free society.

In my thirties, I was blessed to work at Herman Miller, a Fortune 500 global office furniture company, under the leadership and mentorship of Max De Pree, CEO and Chairman of the Board. Max led the company with a powerful *shared* vision and *shared* values that enabled us to achieve extraordinary results *and* make a positive difference in the lives of our employees, customers, families, communities, and the environment, a story I will share with you in this book (Chapter 7).

Next, I served in President Bill Clinton's administration, as Director of the Federal Quality Institute. I found DreamMakers in the US government in pursuit of creating "a government that works better and costs less." I saw people take on the incredibly difficult task of transforming some of the most rigid, complex, and dysfunctional bureaucracies in the world into highly functioning, customer-centered organizations. I also saw people come alive and reconnect with their passion for public service and servant leadership.

Finally, after having worked in almost every sector in diverse roles, I decided to follow my dream, my passion; I found the courage to put my personal vision and values to work and started my own business in 1995. I leaped into the world of entrepreneurship, serving as a transformation catalyst for businesses, organizations, and communities seeking to put their vision and values to work to create a better future for all of their stakeholders. To this day, in an era wrought with global conflicts, failing institutions, and fragile economies, I see a growing number of DreamMakers in business, government, nonprofits, and communities co-creating a brand new world. They are working to create a world where people can thrive, businesses can prosper, and the planet can flourish.

About this book

The stories you are about to read are about *DreamMakers: Innovating for the Greater Good*. I shine a light on world-shaping thought leaders, business innovators, social entrepreneurs, and cross-sector, cross-discipline initiatives and global movements that are collaborating to create a flourishing world. These generous people share their results, what they are learning, and how they are innovating for the greater good *and* making their personal hopes and dreams come true.

Their compelling stories are instructive as well as inspirational. They share the defining moments in their lives that shaped their insights, actions, and decisions that set them on their journey. They share the actions they are taking to help transform their organizations and communities to enable them to innovate for the greater good. They show us that by taking personal responsibility to change our lives, our businesses, and our communities, we contribute to co-creating a better world.

Each conversation is guided by seven topics of inquiry to give a common context for these highly diverse stories.

1. Highest aspiration: the DreamMaker's vision

2. Core values: what matters to them most in life

3. Defining moments that set them on their path to innovating for the greater good

4. Major milestones, decisions, actions and results

5. Challenges and obstacles along the way

6. Important lessons and greatest discoveries

7. How their journey has impacted their lives

As you explore these DreamMakers' stories, I invite you to join the conversation and to contribute your ideas, talents, and energy to making our world a better place. While the media, politicians, and many possessed by fear are preoccupied with messages and images of violence, hate, and the threat of global destruction, there is a rapidly rising global movement of people who are actively reimagining and redesigning a new and better world. Like water, this movement is quietly but powerfully rising into a global tsunami of people co-creating a world where people and the planet can flourish.

This book is about hope, intended for all who are seeking to help create a better future for themselves and our world. It is for people who sense on an intuitive level that we are living in an unprecedented time in which to make a tremendous difference to our world. It is also for people looking for inspiration, insights, and innovative ideas to reshape their lives, businesses, institutions, organizations, and communities and to renew the planet that sustains us. This book is especially for those who choose to accept the personal responsibility and assume the leadership to help create a flourishing world.

Acknowledgments

Thank you:

To my mentor Max De Pree: thank you for your caring, honest guidance over the past 35 years. I have been blessed to have you in my life. I consider you my second father and a dear friend. My father launched me, and you helped me to navigate through the challenging journey of becoming an authentic leader. You are a gift to my spirit and I love you.

Frances Hesselbein: thank you for always reminding me that *To Serve is to Live*. You are a beautiful, exemplary model of *servant leadership*. You have inspired hundreds of thousands of people, especially the youth. You live by Ralf Emerson's quote "Be an opener of doors for such has come after thee." Most of all, thank you for a beautiful friendship over the past 26 years.

To my dear friend Randi Skaamedal: thank you for always being present to listen when I needed to talk, laugh, and cry and for your constant concern for my wellbeing. You are an amazing woman, and a powerful *DreamMaker* in your own right. I deeply treasure our friendship.

To the fearless, inspiring *DreamMakers* in this book and around the world: thank you for standing up, speaking out, and lending your hearts, minds, and unique gifts to transforming our world into a place where *all* people and the planet have the opportunity to flourish.

Note: Some passages in the Introduction and the chapters entitled "My journey through Camelot: A Herman Miller Story" and "We The People" have been previously published by the author in her blog "And The Good News Is..." (http://michelehunt.blogspot.com/2011/06/and-good-news-is-compelling-reasons-for.html), as well as in the Huffington Post, and have been developed for this book.

Introduction: the new definition of success

There is rapidly growing recognition that it is time for a new story for the future of humankind. The old story, where the central plot is that money and power define success, is fundamentally flawed. History has repeatedly proven that this story simply does not work. It causes pain, suffering, and fear; it destroys life and our planet; and it dampens the human spirit. In this narrative, those oppressed by the money–power society inevitably rebel, take over, and sadly repeat the same destructive cycle. We have been living and reliving George Orwell's *Animal Farm* allegory since the beginning of civilization. We have played out the win–lose, conquer or be conquered scenario, and now most people understand that this approach to winning is not sustainable, meaningful, or fun. The opportunity to co-create win–win scenarios by innovating for the greater good is not just a beautiful dream, it is a necessity if people and the planet are to survive and ultimately flourish.

It is time for fundamental systemic change. It is widely understood that the foundation of all that we used to hold sacred has been shaken. Governments, businesses, religions, organizations, communities, the natural environment, and people are all vulnerable. The long-held traditions and institutions that used to guide us in the past are struggling with their own relevancy. Technology has rocketed us into the future with no maps to help us navigate this

FIGURE 0.1   The United Nations Sustainable Development Goals: the new reference point for success

uncharted territory. In addition to these seemingly insurmountable challenges, the proliferation of corporatism and the growing chasm between the rich and the poor is eroding democracy, and the greatest social experiment of all civilizations is now threatened. Democracy's fundamental core values, "government of the people, by the people, for the people," is losing ground. Profit has become the single aim for most businesses, and wealth is becoming concentrated in less than 1% of the global population. These developments have created monumental social and environmental problems that are putting our very existence in danger. It is becoming apparent to most that the plethora of problems we are experiencing are symptoms of obsolete beliefs and old systems breaking down under the weight of a growing awareness that radical, fundamental change is needed.

While there is widespread agreement that we are living in an unprecedented time of change, chaos, and pervasive conflicts, we are also living in an era of amazing technological innovations and stunning new discoveries. This paradoxical reality is fertile ground for us to reconceptualize and create a brand new world. We are beginning to understand that "We The People" can and must change the world. This is awakening us to a whole new level of accountability and responsibility, especially when it comes to the root cause of our problems—how we define success. To change the current trajectory will require a different economic model, one that does not fit neatly within our prevailing narrow interpretation of capitalism.

Simon Mainwaring believes we must put people and the planet first. In his book *We First*,[1] he proposes a compelling argument why we must alter the current free-market system from destructive capitalism to sustainable capitalism. He offers a new vision to "transform the entire private sector—corporations and consumers alike—into a force for global renewal." Mainwaring believes that "We First" is neither anti-capitalist nor anti-wealth. It is "pro-prosperity." He defines prosperity as "well-being for all" and believes that, in the long view, serving everyone's interest also serves our own.

Being successful in the 21st century will require a new economic model and a new way of doing business, a model of achieving success that is more inclusive, collaborative, transparent, and highly integrated; one that values people, community, and the planet as much as it values profit. The new business culture embraces the study and pursuit of mindfulness practices including reflection, meditation, whole-systems thinking, and appreciative inquiry, to enable all stakeholders in society to grow and flourish. It requires us all to personally and collectively continue to pursue our quest to understand the myriad of connections, interdependences, and untapped potential of this great web of life.

This enlightened way of viewing success is not a new idea. It has been evolving over time. Much of the thinking that influenced this new definition of success has emerged from the great thought leaders of the 20th century who dared to challenge business and government leaders to be thoughtful and to bear the responsibility of creating more collaborative, integrated, humane environments that value people, communities and the planet. Some of the most influential thought leaders who helped to plant the seeds of this movement include: Peter Drucker, management thought leader

1   Mainwaring, S. (2011). *We First: How Brands and Consumers Use Social Media to Build a Better World.* New York: Palgrave Macmillan.

and author of *Post-Capitalist Society*; Willis Harman, futurist and author of *Global Mind Change: The Promise of the 21st Century*; Dr. W. Edwards Deming, the father of the Quality Management movement; Warren Bennis, eminent scholar on leadership and author of *Beyond Leadership: Balancing Economics, Ethics and Ecology*; Max De Pree, former CEO and Chairman of Herman Miller and author of *Leadership is an Art*; Charles Handy, philosopher and author of *The Age of Unreason*; Peter Senge, author of *The Fifth Discipline: The Art and Practice of the Learning Organization* and *The Necessary Revolution: How Individuals and Organizations are Working Together to Create a Sustainable World*; Margaret Wheatley, author of *Leadership and the New Science: Discovering Order in a Chaotic World*, and Malcolm Gladwell, author of *The Tipping Point*. Today this holistic, collaborative, caring way of doing business is firmly embedded in the minds, hearts, and imagination of the best and brightest people on the planet. The majority of people in our world, if given the choice, would choose to lend their time, energy, and creative talents to pursuits that exemplify this approach to success.

The good news is that there is a rapidly growing number of people around the world that are embracing a bold new positive vision of "A world in which businesses and other organizations can excel, people can thrive, and nature can flourish."[2] The challenges we face are of such magnitude that people are not waiting for governments, global leaders, gurus, or a miracle to save them. People are feeling a heighted since of urgency, which is moving them to self-organize to make change happen. Forward-thinking entrepreneurs, businesses, and communities of like-minded people are finding the courage to come together to work on solving some of the world's most pressing problems. They are stepping out of their day-to-day parochial view of life and taking actions to innovate for the greater good. People are discovering that their hopes and dreams of love, health, peace, and prosperity for their families and their communities can be realized

[2]   Laszlo, C. and Brown, J.S. (2014) *Flourishing Enterprise: The New Spirit of Business*. Stanford, CA: Stanford Busiess Books, p. 60.

when they see themselves as a part of a greater whole, and they work for the greater good.

This new consciousness is igniting a hopeful global movement born out of the deeply held shared values that resonate within most of us. People are openly and passionately expressing their desire to connect with others, express themselves and be heard. The explosion of social networking through rapidly evolving internet technology gives powerful examples of people hungry to connect with others around ideas and concerns they hold in common. These communities of like-minded people are redefining ways of being together; moving from hierarchal, exclusive, separated constructs to inclusive communities that flourish on the flow of information and ideas around common interest. While the media choose to focus on the abuses and destructive groups on the internet, there are far more positive communities creating new thinking and new possibilities and generating new actions for positive change that impact us all. A beautiful new definition of success is emerging that is inspiring people to join movements to transform our world by innovating and solving problems with the greater good in mind.

It is estimated that over 3 billion people have access to the internet today. This number has increased tenfold since 1999 and, by many accounts, most people in the world will be digitally connected in the next five years. Eric Schmidt, Executive Chairman of Google, asserts "By the end of the decade, everyone on Earth will be connected."[3] Although many call his prediction optimistic there is little argument that the majority of the world will be online by 2020. Cisco Systems has a compelling TV ad that poses an intriguing question: "What if the next big thing isn't a thing at all, it's lots of things, all waking up becoming part of the global phenomenon we call the internet of everything?" It goes on to say, "It's going to be amazing and exciting and maybe, most remarkably, not that far away."

3   Schmidt, E. [EricSmith] (2013, April 12). By the end of the decade, everyone on Earth will be connected [Tweet]. Retrieved from https://twitter.com/ericschmidt/status/322942312093192193?lang=en-gb.

I believe this phenomenon is becoming a powerful, hopeful global movement that is driving deep, fundamental, positive change. People are breaking out of the patterns of cynicism, hopelessness, and despair and discovering that by collaborating with others around a shared vision of the future we can create a new reality. Like the DreamMakers profiled in this book, people are coming up with bold, innovative ideas on how to change their communities and our world. They are not asking for permission or forgiveness but rather putting their ideas to work. This new consciousness is rippling across our world almost as fast as technology can carry it. Rapidly evolving internet technology has become a powerful tool for social, environmental, and political action—and it is unstoppable!

It is impossible to calculate the impact this new consciousness will have on our world in the next five years; I believe it will be enormous, and I am not alone. A growing number of people believe this is a historical game-changer never before seen in the history of humankind. I used to think that the issues in our world are of such enormous magnitude that only the most optimistic, powerful, and visionary leaders could even dream of tackling them. Crushing poverty, hate, prejudice, environmental degradation, and pervasive conflicts was reserved for the mighty and the powerful. But the "pockets of hope" that I am witnessing, where ordinary people are banding together and doing extraordinary things, have taught me that the impossible is possible. One young man in a Puerto Rico community in Chicago expressed his view of the future: "There are all of these pockets of hope developing all over the world. Pretty soon there will be so many pockets of hope, that there will no longer be pockets, it will just be."

This hopeful vision of our future is not an impossible dream—it is an insight into the capacity of human potential. If we look at all the amazing things people have created throughout history, they were all considered impossible by the status quo at some time in their development. Like the DreamMakers in this book, I believe the seeds that hold a vision for a new and better world lie within each of us, waiting for the right time and conditions to germinate, grow, and blossom. I believe that **innovating for the greater good** is an idea whose time has come. It is a movement that is rapidly rising and on the threshold of flourishing. It is our time, our right, and our responsibility to collectively come together to create a brand new world.

> A movement is a collective state of mind, a public and common understanding that the future can be created, not simply experience or endured (Max De Pree, Former CEO and Chairman, Herman Miller, Inc.).

Part 1
Businesses as agents of world benefit

David Cooperrider, founder and Chair, Fowler
Center for Business as an Agent of World Benefit

1
Fowler Center for Business as an Agent of World Benefit

> Imagine a world of nine billion people with clean water, quality food, affordable housing and education, top-tier medical care, ubiquitous clean energy, dignified opportunities, thriving economies, and global peace and security (David Cooperrider, founder and Chair, Fowler Center Business as an Agent of World Benefit).

David Cooperrider believes deeply in this audacious, bodacious vision for our world. He is founder and Chair of the Fowler Center for Business as an Agent of World Benefit, at the Weatherhead School of Management, Case Western Reserve University. David is also the co-creator of Appreciative Inquiry.

The Fowler Center for Business as an Agent of World Benefit's mission is "To advance new knowledge for transforming the world's most complex problems into business opportunities for industry-leading innovation and world-shaping benefit." The Fowler Center is also part of a rapidly growing, powerful global movement; a network of businesses and networks around the globe that are working to create a world where people can thrive, business can prosper, and the planet can flourish. In the 21st century, this vision has taken root and is beginning to blossom into what many believe will soon become a worldwide phenomenon. David's journey to create the Fowler Center has had a significant impact on this movement. He has been on a quest to help advance this vision for 29 years.

It was in 1987 when David had an epiphany while having a conversation with Willis Harman, the renowned futurist and former president of the Institute of Noetic Sciences, who studied global systems. Harman was sharing his scenarios on the trajectory of the world's future, and the only scenario that was optimistic was one where businesses emerged as a powerful, creative force for good. David vividly remembers that defining moment: "My meeting Willis Harman in his office was like opening the doors in my mind." The seeds of the Fowler Center for Business as an Agent of World Benefit were firmly planted that day.

The 1999 gathering of the World Economic Forum in Davos, Switzerland, may have been the tipping point for this movement. At this historic event, United Nations (UN) Secretary-General Kofi Annan challenged the leaders from business, labor, and civil society to collaborate to solve the most challenging problems facing our world. Kofi Annan sent an invitation to world business and civic leaders: "Let us choose to unite the power of markets with the strength of universal ideals. Let us choose to reconcile the creative forces of private entrepreneurship with the needs of the disadvantaged and the requirements of future generations" (Kofi Annan reported by David Cooperrider).

Inspired by that World Economic Forum, David and others at the Weatherhead School of Management at Case Western Reserve University launched a world inquiry into business as an agent of world benefit. This research project created a data bank of stories of profitable business innovations in environmental sustainability and social entrepreneurship. During that research it became apparent to David and the research team that a world-shaping movement was emerging. After 2,000 interviews they realized that they were documenting a revolution.

After the horrific acts of terrorism in the USA on September 11, 2001, David felt a tremendous sense of urgency to help advance this movement. He solicited the advice of Peter Drucker, the management thought leader, who confirmed David's belief that there were urgent and compelling reasons to help accelerate Business as an Agent of World Benefit into a global vision. In *Management: Tasks,*

Responsibilities, Practices (1973)[1] Drucker cited examples of companies, including Sears and Ford, that had figured out how to build a business by taking on social ills. And late in his life, Drucker was still singing the same song. "Every single social and global issue of our day," he declared, "is a business opportunity in disguise."

In 2004, Secretary-General Kofi Annan invited David to design and facilitate a summit on global corporate citizenship at the United Nations. At this historic summit, Kofi Annan and 500 business leaders came together to explore ways that business, academia, and civil society could work together to make globalization work for everyone.

As a result of this summit, Case Western Reserve University, in cooperation with the Academy of Management and the UN Global Compact, created the Global Forum for Business as an Agent for World Benefit. At their 2006 Forum the strategic sponsors developed the platform for an ongoing triennial meeting of businesses who embraced this vision. The delegates came to the shared agreement that business had the opportunity to be one of the most creative forces on the planet; they collectively proclaimed: "The 21st century can become an unprecedented century of sustainable innovation where businesses can excel, people can thrive, and nature can flourish." In 2014, the Global Forum for Business as an Agent for World Benefit held the third Global Forum, Flourish & Prosper, where over 500 corporate leaders and academic thought leaders came together to learn, share their stories and to collectively co-create ways to advance this movement.

Chuck and Char Fowler so deeply believe that businesses should **do good, do well,** they made an extraordinary gift of $7.5 million dollars to establish the Fowler Center for Business as an Agent of World Benefit at the Weatherhead School of Management at Case Western Reserve University and appointed David as director. Chuck Fowler served as Chairman of the Board of Trustees at Case Western Reserve and is the founder and Chairman of Fairmount Santrol,

---

1   Drucker, P. (1973). *Management: Tasks, Responsibilities, Practices.* New York: Harper Collins.

FIGURE 1.1   Char and Chuck Fowler

a producer of sand-based products based in Cleveland Ohio. The company is committed to helping to create sustainable futures for their people, the planet and all their stakeholders. Chuck has practiced these values for 40 years and he is committed to spreading them to businesses around the world. See Chapter 6 for more on Fairmount Santrol and Chuck Fowler.

AIM2Flourish

In response to David and Chuck's vision and investment, the Fowler Center launched a global learning initiative to discover and recognize business innovations that are doing good and doing well. It started in 2012 with an OpenIDEO global crowdsourcing event. They invited people across cultures around the world to share their stories to help identify and celebrate businesses that are innovating for world benefit. People from 100 countries contributed their insights and ideas. This inquiry evolved into AIM2Flourish, a global process to identify, recognize, celebrate, and shine a light on the best-of-the-best business innovation stories that serve the greater good.

The mission of AIM2Flourish is "To connect students to 100,000 ingenious business leaders, to reveal their business innovations for good." Their vision is that "Future business leaders solve the UN Global Goals for a flourishing world." This initiative is co-sponsored by the UN Global Compact Principles for Responsible Management (PRME), a network of more than 600 leading business schools and management education institutions from 80 countries around the world, the Globally Responsible Leadership Initiative (GRLI), and AACSB International, the accreditation organization for 777 management schools.

> My biggest dream is for us is to make a positive difference in the world, and to use the Fowler Center for Business as an Agent of World Benefit as an avenue to wake up businesses to enable them to see the challenges we face with the environment and the planet; and to figure out what we need to do for people and the planet to survive and flourish (Chuck Fowler, Chair, Case Western Reserve University Board of Directors, and Chairman, Fairmount Santrol).

AIM2Flourish has a unique approach to finding and reporting on business innovations that are helping to create a flourishing world. Business school students take the ownership for this phase of the process. Working through their professors, they seek out, discover, and interview these business leaders. The students use Appreciative Inquiry, a positive change methodology that focuses on identifying the strengths of an organization, to guide their work. They submit those stories online to AIM2Flourish.com using social media to spread the word about businesses innovation for good. This professor-facilitated process is a tremendous learning opportunity for the students, professors, and business leaders.

> AIM2Flourish.com is the world's first student-led global learning platform, showcasing business innovations that solve humanity's greatest challenges. Business students around the world are using Appreciative Inquiry (strength-based

interviews) and the UN's 17 Sustainable Development Goals to search out and report on world-changing innovations.

…

We'll celebrate the best-of-the-best business innovation stories in June 2017 at the Fourth Global Forum on Discovering Flourishing Enterprise. This initiative represents an unparalleled opportunity to dynamically connect students, business leaders, management schools, media makers, and investors across geographies, generations, and industries (Author's interview with Roberta Baskin, Executive Director, AIM2Flourish).

AIM2Flourish is inspiring the next generation of business leaders and business school educators to embrace the concept of businesses as an agent of world benefit. Here is what some of the AIM2Flourish students and professors are saying about their experience with this learning process:

Having an opportunity to conduct an interview and probe a particular innovation and flourishing story is already a great learning experience for us. Our paradigms somehow shifted toward a sustainable direction of conducting business (in the future) wherein social innovation will form the nuclei of our business models. Writing the story highly inspired us. That in itself is already a huge reward for us. (Bernard Bairoy, Student, IPMI International Business School, Indonesia).

I have found myself speaking of AIM2Flourish stories to family, friends, grandchildren, students, colleagues, whenever the opportunity presents itself. It's an energizing and meaningful experience for the students, the business leaders who share their stories and for me to be a part of this world changing effort (Professor George Dionne, IESDE School of Management, Mexico).

The idea of the project itself, the flourishing idea, really touched their hearts, and made them really look at the subject, not as a matter of passing the grades or not, but more like, "ah, this is my calling!" (Professor Amelia Naim Indrajaya, IPMI International Business School, Indonesia).

Here is a peek at a few of the stories that students are discovering and reporting from around the world:

- **Lucky Iron Fish.** Responding to iron deficiency, a pervasive condition for 25% of the population in Cambodia that can lead to severe physical illness, impaired cognitive ability, and death, an entrepreneur created a simple solution: the Lucky Iron Fish, a piece of iron shaped like a fish to be used in cooking pots to increase iron levels in the Cambodian population.

- **PT Tirta Marta: tapioca plastic bags.** An Indonesian-based company is moving from producing plastic bags that take 500 years to degrade to making plastic bags that degrade in two weeks. Its affordable, eco-friendly bags are made from tapioca, which comes from the cassava root grown in the region and which the company sources from local tapioca cooperatives. It is making a positive social, economic and environmental impact on its community.

- **PT Holcim: rice husk for fuel.** An Indonesian company is substituting fossil fuel coal with agricultural waste to generate fuel. It projects savings of 500,000 tons of CO_2 each year for the next ten years.

- **Divine Chocolate: fairtrade chocolate.** The company is co-owned by Kuapa Kokoo, a farmers' cooperative in Ghana that provides the cocoa for Divine, the first-ever farmer-owned Fairtrade chocolate bar. The 85,000 members share in the profits of the company and have a voice in the direction of the company.

AIM2Flourish is growing exponentially. It started in the spring of 2015 with 24 professors from 19 countries and has grown to over 100 colleges and universities. As of December 2016 more than 1,600 professors, students, and citizens from 56 countries are participating in this exciting global learning initiative; and it is still in its infancy. "It's about today's companies and their partners unleashing disruptive innovations that address humankind's greatest transitional opportunities, on the pathway from non-sustainability to sustainability—to a world-wide state of flourishing" (David Cooperrider).

Jay Coen Gilbert, cofounder, B Lab

2

B Corporations: business as a force for good

Certified

B

Corporation

I sit on the Advisory Board of the Fowler Center for Business as an Agent of World Benefit. It was during a board meeting in 2012 that I first heard about B Lab and its innovative business model, the B Corporation (B Corp). There were about 600 companies who were in the B Corp community at that time; today there are more than 2,000 in 50 countries from 130 industries. They have one unifying goal: **people using business as a force for good™**. This idea has been a passion of mine since I worked at Herman Miller in the 1980s and back then we felt we were all alone. Many of our peer executives from other companies disagreed with our people-centered participative management system, our commitment to be good stewards of the environment, and our engagement in communities; some went as far as calling us socialist. They believed that the single aim of business was maximizing shareholder value and they were slaves of that aim. So I was elated to talk with Jay Coen Gilbert, a cofounder of B Lab, and learn more about B Corps and his personal story that led him to commit to going on this journey.

1,929 Companies, 50 Countries, 130 Industries, 1 Unifying Goal

FIGURE 2.1   B Corp: "Using business as a force for good"

It is always fun to talk to people who are passionate about their vision, especially when their vision is big, bold and world-changing. Although I found Jay to be incredibly humble, his passion for the community of B Corps was contagious. I left the interview hopeful and excited, because there was tangible proof that business leaders are waking up to the powerful potential they have to co-create a world where people can thrive, business can prosper, and the planet can flourish.

I learned that Jay Coen Gilbert and his two cofounders, Bart Houlahan and Andrew Kassoy (Fig. 2.2), are powerful catalysts and enablers of a growing global movement that is clearly a shift in consciousness; a shift from the traditional view of business to a whole new mindset. This movement, in fact, may be the force that saves the world from environmental, social, and economic devastation. These brilliant innovators have not only served as effective advocates for a new business model based on a highly inclusive definition of success, they have also created the infrastructure, tools and processes that enable businesses to make the transition from the narrow view of profit maximization to business as a force for good.

These social entrepreneurs are helping leaders that are waking up to this enlightened business model to manage and measure the impact they have on all their stakeholders: people, communities, and the environment, as well as shareholders. They are shining examples of DreamMakers, innovating for the greater good.

FIGURE 2.2   The cofounders of B Lab: Jay Coen Gilbert, Bart Houlahan, and Andrew Kassoy

Their vision is that "One day all companies compete not only to be the best in the world, but the Best for the World®." To that end, they developed B Lab, a nonprofit organization that serves this global movement of entrepreneurs. B Lab, itself an innovation, is what I would call the research and development (R & D) arm of this movement. They have developed an impressive suite of highly effective, innovative strategies, structures, processes, and tools that enable companies to transform this shared vision into reality, including:

- **Certified B Corporations.** A global community of companies that meet the highest standards of verified overall social and environmental performance, public transparency, and legal accountability. "We need the kind of businesses that B Corps represent, those conscious of responsibilities to all our diverse stakeholders: employees, customers, communities and, not least, the health of the natural systems that undergird our economy" (Rose Marcario, CEO, Patagonia).

- **Benefit Corporation.** An innovative corporate legal structure authorized by 30 US states and the District of Columbia that aligns the interests of business with those of society by expanding the fiduciary duty of corporate directors to consider the impact of their decisions not only on share-holders, but also on workers, the community, and the environment.

- **B Impact Assessment and B Analytics.** Tools to help businesses, investors, and institutions to manage their impact with as much rigor as their profits.

- **B Corp Champions Retreat.** The global gathering of the B Corps to explore and plan collective actions they can take to help create a better world.

- **B Ambassadors.** Professional athletes and other celebrities that are supportive of the B Corp movement. Their voices bring public attention to the B Corp movement and help to reinforce the concept of business as a force for good.

  > I'm really proud to be a B Corp ambassador. I think it stands for the most ultimate change I want to see on the planet: a global movement where business is a force for good. And to me, it's the only solution (Chanelle Sladics, professional snowboarder).

- **B Impact Fellows.** A fellowship program that B Lab launched in 2015. There were 400 applicants for 12 fellowship positions, which made the inaugural class of fellows more selective than Harvard University. They selected both recent graduates and mid-career professionals interested in working for businesses that are a force for good and who demonstrated past and potential leadership abilities in helping companies create value for their employees, their communities and the environment. These fellows were trained by B Lab for five weeks and then sent out to partner with community organizations to help companies manage and measure their impact.

  > We are creating sort of an AmeriCorps for the impact economy. This year, for example, most of the Fellows are working for a partnership we established with the New York City Economic Development Corporation called "Best of NYC." It is a multi-year campaign to invite all small businesses to compete to be the best for New York—best for New York

workers and the best for the city neighborhoods (Jay Coen Gilbert).

- **B the Change Media.** A media company launched by B Lab whose mission is to build the world's largest engaged audience of people with a passion for using business as a force for good. Like a rolling stone for business, it hopes to accelerate the cultural shift under way in which business—as music did in the late 1960s—has become a part of our identity and a tool for social change. It launched in June 2016 and will include digital content, a print magazine, and events.

-  B Lab's annual **Best for the World** List, which has been covered by Forbes, Inc., *Wall Street Journal*, Fast Company, *The New York Times*, and numerous other business media outlets, recognizes those companies scoring in the top 10% of all B Corps globally.

Companies that have joined the B Corp community are some of the most innovative and life-nurturing companies in the world; they are from highly diverse industries from around the world. Some of these recognized in the Best for the World List include: Australian Ethical Investment, investment advising; Beneficial State Bank, credit provider, US; Caravela Coffee, Colombia; CarShare Atlantic, transportation, Canada; Juhudi Kilimo, credit provider, Kenya; Off-Grid Solutions/WakaWaka, solar power, Netherlands; Sunrise Banks, finance, US; TriCiclos, waste management, Chile; Échale! a tu casa, construction, Mexico; TIVENCA, R&D, Venezuela; HCA, healthcare, US; Impact First Investments, investment advising, Israel; One Earth Designs, electronics, Hong Kong; Piedmont Biofuels, energy generation, US; and Telecom Development Company, telecommunications, Afghanistan.

Kickstarter, the highly successful online crowdfunding website, whose mission is "To bring creative projects to life," became a B Corporation in September 2015:

> Kickstarter is excited to join a growing list of forward-thinking organizations—like Patagonia and This American

Life—that have taken the big step to become a Benefit Corporation. While only about .01% of all American businesses have done this, we believe that can and will change in the coming years. More and more voices are rejecting business as usual, and the pursuit of profit above all (Kickstarter Press Release, September 21, 2015).

B Lab not only serves the community of B Corps, but also aspires to help all companies interested in being a force for good to understand the tremendous benefits it brings to all their stakeholders. To help make that possible, Ryan Honeyman, a sustainability consultant from B Corp LIFT Economy, teamed up with another B Corp, Berrett-Koehler Publishers, to write *The B Corp Handbook*.[1] The handbook website displays some impressive endorsements: "The B Corp Handbook shows how using business as a force for good can be better for consumers, employees, local communities, the environment, and your company's long-term bottom line (Tony Hsieh, *New York Times* bestselling author of *Delivering Happiness* and CEO, Zappos.co); and "My guess is that this new idea [benefit corporations] will turn out to be a winner, that will yield some of our most profitable corporations because of the employee and community support they will inspire" (Robert Shiller, 2013 Nobel Laureate in Economics, and Professor, Yale University).

Meet Jay Cohen Gilbert

Jay's highest aspiration

We need to create a more inclusive economy that works for everybody. For that to happen business must operate differently in the 21st century than in the 20th century. That means taking on the responsibility and seizing the opportunity to bring our whole selves to work everyday—to get connected to a higher purpose. That can be through the products and services we create, the types of customers we serve, or the way in which we make or distribute our products. The North Star of business should

[1]   Honeyman, R. (2014). *The B Corps Handbook: How to Use Business as a Force for Good*. Oakland, CA: Berrett-Koehler.

be the positive impact we can create, using profit as the fuel for, not the destination of, our journey.

Business is the result of choices we make, and those choses can have a more or less positive impact on the world. The big transformation we are seeing is a culture shift that redefines success in business—where success is measured not only by the money that you make, but also by the difference you make in the world, and we measure that difference with as much rigor and care as we do profits. As a result of the choices we make in where we work, in whom we invest, in what we buy, in how we run our businesses, there will be less inequality, less poverty, a healthier environment, and stronger, more vibrant, and connected communities. This is possible as we recognize our interdependence and that the purpose of economic growth is human fulfillment, not just wealth creation.

In our picture of success, all companies are not B Corps, but all companies behave like B Corps. The result would be that there would be more jobs for people with disabilities, there would be more women-led and minority-led businesses, there would be more businesses working with suppliers from low-income communities, and everybody would earn a living wage. When all companies behave like B Corps, businesses would be zero waste, net positive in their carbon footprint and we would have made a successful transition from a fossil-fuel-based economy to a renewable-energy economy. All of those things can happen and can happen more quickly if business is driving that change instead of resisting or being indifferent to managing for impact, not just for profit.

Obviously there are plenty of places the market doesn't go, but when we are at our best as a society, business, government, and civil society are in balance in seeking the common objective of improving the quality of life for all, and making sure that future generations have the opportunity to enjoy that quality of life. Right now, if feels as if we have become out of balance. The B Corp movement is trying to restore a proper balance between business and the other elements of a good society. We need business to resume its proper role in society as a creator of community health, not just a creator of personal wealth.

DECLARATION OF INTERDEPENDENCE

We envision a global economy that uses business as a force for good.

This economy is comprised of a new type of corporation – the B Corporation – Which is purpose-driven and creates benefit for all stakeholders, not just shareholders.

As B Corporations and leaders of this emerging economy, we believe:

> That we must be the change we seek in the world.

> That all business ought to be conducted as if people and place mattered.

> That, through their products, practices, and profits, businesses should aspire to do no harm and benefit all.

> To do so requires that we act with the understanding that we are each dependent upon another and thus responsible for each other and future generations.

FIGURE 2.3   B Corp's Declaration of Interdependence

Core values

My highest aspiration is that we live in a way that recognizes our interdependence. If I can live that way, and if business can operate that way, we would be doing nothing more difficult than applying the Golden Rule in all of our business relationships. The Golden Rule shows up in almost every faith and wisdom tradition around the world; it is incredibly simple but very difficult to achieve. So for me, the core value is that we are all interdependent and that each human being has inherent dignity. We need to approach our relationships from that core understanding. If we do that, we will treat each other fairly and with a long-term view of a mutually beneficial relationship rather than a singularly "winning" transaction. If I can do that in my personal life today, better than I did yesterday, that's a big step forward. If we can create a global community of businesses that shares that objective, then maybe these businesses can be drum majors in a much bigger parade of people that are using business as a force for good. That's why the founding document of the B Corp community is the Declaration of Interdependence (Fig. 2.3).

This document is the result of inspiration that came from a lot of different places around the world, and over a long period of time. It has obvious references to the US Declaration of Independence, but we also embrace Gandhi's invocation that we try to "be the change we want to see in the world." In addition to seeking freedom from imperialism, Gandhi was a huge advocate for economic systems that created pathways out of poverty for marginalized populations and communities. Our focus on "conducting businesses as if people and place matter" is a reference to the seminal work of the British economist E.F. Schumacher, *Small is Beautiful.*[2] The reference to the highest aspiration of business "to do no harm and benefit all," is a reference to both the Golden Rule, which come from many different faith traditions, and the Tao Te Ching, a famous Taoist text from China.

This is what we stand for and yet we recognize that we all fall short of realizing these values every day, but that doesn't mean that it is not the appropriate North Star to guide us. We aspire to live this document in our personal lives and in our work.

Defining moments

I think everyone has their own particular journey and I'm not different than most people in that we are all a product of our environment, particularly our family. Both of my parents were entrepreneurs so I have a little bit of that DNA in me. My parents ran their businesses in ways that were consistent with some of the principles that we see in the B Corp community.

My mom cofounded Gilbert Tweed, the largest women- and minority-owned executive search firm in the country back in the 1970s. I can't remember a white male in the place at the time, and that was back when the old boys' network dominated that industry and corporate America generally. In particular, she created career paths for women both within her organization and in corporate America at a time when those career

2   Schumacher, E. (1973). *Small is Beautiful: A Study of Economics as if People Mattered.* London: Blond & Briggs.

paths did not exist. I learned a lot about the importance of inclusion for our culture and for business success from my mom.

My dad ran an architecture firm for a long time and used that platform in the 1980s to create an organization called Architects for Social Responsibility during the Cold War. President Regan was in office and we were all concerned about the "Evil Empire" and nuclear threats. My dad was embarrassed and ashamed that he sat out the civil rights movement as a student and young professional in New York in the 1960s. He vowed if he ever got the opportunity to engage in a big issue again he would not let it go by a second time. So with his children entering their teenage years, and with what he viewed as a potential existential threat to their future and the future of his grandchildren, he used his business as a platform to organize the leaders in his industry around disarmament and building a better relationship with the Soviet Union. He really stuck his neck out and sacrificed his own business to take a stand on something he thought was incredibly important. A decade later, I had graduated from college and had worked at McKinsey so he sent me to Russia to see if there were partnership opportunities. His was the first American firm to work in the Soviet Union and later he became the first American to be inducted into the Moscow Institute of Architects. He was most proud that he was elected by his peers as a Fellow in the American Institute of Architects in recognition of the work he did to organize the industry around this issue.

I learned a great deal from both parents: from my mom on gender issues and the role of inclusion in business and from my dad on not only using your business as a platform but also choosing what business you are in, or not. He was offered a job to design the work spaces for an engineering company that he learned was working on a guidance system for weapons of mass destruction. It was a very big contract and yet he decided he would not take it. He realized it was architects that had designed the gas chambers in Auschwitz. He had a choice and he chose to follow his values. My parents, by example, really influenced me so when I started my own business I tried to incorporate those values. My mom passed in 2001 and five years later my dad passed. Not surprisingly, the combination of events, coupled with the birth of our first child, made me question if I was using whatever gifts and privilege I had to the highest and best use.

Our first company was AND 1—a basketball apparel and footwear company. Bart Houlahan was the president and Andrew Kassoy an early investor. Over a decade or so, the business was successful and we were fortunate enough to be able to sell it relatively early in our lives so we had plenty of room to grow and plenty of time to make a contribution to the world. After a lot of dialogue, we figured the highest use of our time was to work out how we could support all these incredible entrepreneurs and investors we had met who were interested in doing more with the money they had made than just making more money. Then the question became how we could be of most use to them.

So in 2006 we three college buddies came to the conclusion that the biggest thing we could do was to try to help accelerate this movement of people striving to use business as a force for good. This manifested through a nonprofit called B Lab, which is doing several different things to help support and accelerate that movement. B Lab certifies for-profit companies that meet our rigorous standards of social and environmental performance, accountability, and transparency; they are called B Corps and they are the leaders of this movement. It includes a useful tool, B Impact Assessment, that businesses can use to manage their impact; there are more than 40,000 businesses using it already. It also includes a legal structure that folks can use to make sure they are creating a positive impact over the long term and that's the Benefit Corporation; there are nearly 4,000 benefit corporations in the US. We are working with these three aligned communities of businesses and inviting everybody else to join us. It is a lot more fun and meaningful, and for many, a more profitable way of doing business, if you are trying to both make money and make a difference at the same time.

The most compelling thing for us is always about when the B Corp community comes together to do something that none of the individual businesses, no matter how prominent or successful, could have done alone. That started with the existence of the community itself. The very first time B Corps were talked about in public was when 18 companies got together on a stage in a conference in California and publically declared that they wanted to be a part of creating a community of businesses that distinguished themselves through the higher standards that they met around their overall social and environmental performance. So the first act of leadership was a collective act of leadership. If we did not have that collective credibility, neither B Lab nor B Corps would have been successful. Ultimately the credibility of the B Corp movement is in the quality of the companies that choose to meet these standards voluntarily.

Another example is when this community realized that there were structural changes that needed to be made to US corporate law to be supportive of doing business as a force for good, and that we needed to come together to become a powerful constituency for that legislative change. We drafted new legislation to create a new corporate structure called the benefit corporation and the companies used their relationships in their local communities to pass legislation to support companies that want to create a positive impact, not just a positive return. Today, over 30 states and the District of Columbia have benefit corporation laws When we passed legislation in Delaware, the home of US corporate law, it was a pretty powerful moment. We were with the leaders of the Delaware Bar and the Chief Justice of what amounts to the US Supreme Court for business when the governor signed the bill into law. It was described by the chair of the Delaware Bar as a "seismic shift" in US corporate law, and that did not happen because of B Lab or any individual company; it happened because of the collective action of a community of credible business leaders. These are the types of things that are seminal moments for me, because they represent the power of the collective.

Most important lessons learned

One of the most important lessons we are learning is that this is all about distributive leadership: the importance of giving people the permission to lead and also creating the platforms and programs to help them to lead effectively; whether they are in the C-suite or the loading dock, living in New York or Nairobi. The most important thing we can do is to create a culture of distributive leadership where there is a common vision and that everyone knows that they have the power to achieve that vision through their individual leadership or their role as business leader, consumer, employee, or investor. It's not about us; it's about empowering others. We at B Lab aspire to be servant leaders to help businesses accomplish their goals and people live into their best selves. We bust our butts everyday but we do it because it's fun, meaningful work.

What I learned from Jay Cohen Gilbert

Working at Herman Miller taught me that **doing good and doing well** can be a viable and purposeful business model. I never dreamed, however, that so many CEOs would adopt this mission. Empowered by B Corp tools and support and, most important, by the community of like-minded business leaders, B Corp companies are helping to make the systemic changes needed to enable companies around the world to operate as **a force for good**.

The entrepreneurial spirit and experience of Jay and his fellow cofounders, Bart Houlahan and Andrew Kassoy, gives them a unique perspective on what needs to be done to support the B Corp community. As a result, the number of B Corps have grown into a community of fascinating companies that dare to join, and in some cases lead, the global movement of co-creating a world where people and the planet can flourish.

Maurits Groen, Cofounder, WakaWaka

Archbishop Desmond Tutu

3
WakaWaka: share the sun

WAKA WAKA
share the sun

> We're a social impact company on a mission to provide universal access to the abundant energy of the sun. ... We help people plug into the sun. For power and for light. In an emergency or for play. In the middle of the city or way off the beaten path. ... WakaWaka means "shine bright" in Swahili. We help share the sun (WakaWaka mission statement).

> The future of off-grid countries is indeed bright, thanks to the free, and democratizing solar energy they can now harness. No more noxious, dangerous, CO_2-producing, poor and expensive kerosene for light or diesel for power generation (Maurits Groen, cofounder, WakaWaka).

> By making solar energy accessible to those in need, the WakaWaka Foundation has a positive impact on refugees, victims of natural disasters and epidemics and countless others in need. Together with Kofi Annan, the World Economic Forum Global Shapers and many others I express my deep appreciation for their work across Africa, Asia, the Middle East and Latin America (from a letter to WakaWaka from Archbishop Emeritus Desmond Tutu, Desmond & Leah Tutu Legacy Foundation, 25 August 2014).

On my quest to find businesses that are innovating for the greater good, I came across an article in the *Huffington Post* titled "Without Light, Can There Be Life?" It was written by the cofounders of

WakaWaka, Maurits Groen and Camille van Gestel. They wrote about the 1.2 billion people living without access to electricity as a result of extreme poverty or devastating natural disasters. Their response to this seemingly intractable social issue was to innovate a highly efficient, low-cost, hand-held solar-powered LED light and charger that they named WakaWaka. I was intrigued and discovered from their website that this award-winning device was bringing light and power to over a million people in 43 countries around the world. So I went to the Netherlands to interview Maurits Groen in his Off-Grid Solutions office in Haarlem. As with all the DreamMakers I have met on my journey, Maurits has a powerful purpose in life. He has a compelling global vision of a just world that is rooted in his belief that *all* people and the planet matter. Maurits' personal story is fascinating, inspiring, and instructive.

Maurits Groen, a Dutchman, is a passionate, prolific, self-described "serial sustainable entrepreneur." For the past 25 years he has been a tireless advocate and proponent of social, environmental, and economic sustainability. He founded MGMC, a communication and consultant agency, where he advised businesses, nongovernmental organizations (NGOs) and government on sustainability for over 25 years. In 1980 Maurits helped the Dutch Department of the Environment write the Netherland's first environmental policy. He was chief editor and publisher of *Friends of the Earth Netherlands*. He founded several companies with the mission to advocate sustainability including Greenem and DoTheBrightThing. He also founded a publishing company that was the first to translate US Vice President Al Gore's book, *An Inconvenient Truth*, in 2006. He has produced radio and TV shows, and films on sustainability. He organized the premiers of the films *An Inconvenient Truth*, *The 11th Hour* with Leonardo DiCaprio in 2007, the British documentary *The Age of Stupid* in 2009, and the Dutch film *Silent Snow* in 2011.

In 2010 Maurits and Camille van Gestel won the South African government's international competition to find solutions to reduce the local carbon emissions for the FIFA 2010 World Cup. While in Africa, Maurits had a shocking awakening; he was exposed to the

FIGURE 3.1   An Indonesian household lit by a WakaWaka

plight of people living in **energy poverty**. According to the World
Health Organization, around 3 billion people light, cook, and heat
their homes using open fires and simple stoves burning biomass
(kerosene, wood, animal dung, and crop waste) and coal; 300,000
people die each year from fires; over 4 million people die prema-
turely from illness attributable to the household air pollution from
cooking with solid fuels; and millions more are maimed because
they have to resort to using very dangerous and highly toxic form
of energy.[1] Energy poverty not only has a devastating impact on the
health and well-being of these families, it also impacts the ability of
children living in these communities to have a quality education,
contributes to high crime rates and greatly suppresses the local
economies. One of Maurits' core values is social justice and this
belief moved him beyond sympathy or even empathy for people
living in these heartbreaking conditions; it moved him to act.

In response to this seemingly intractable global social problem, Maurits and Camille put their vision and values to work and
cofounded Off-Grid Solutions and the WakaWaka Foundation, a
business that serves as a powerful force for good. Their business

1   Source: http://www.iea.org/topics/energypoverty/

FIGURE 3.2   Empowering women

created WakaWaka Power, a handheld device that is the most efficient solar-powered LED light and charger in the world. It provides
up to 150 hours of bright LED light on a single charge from the
sun and can charge cell phones, cameras, and "any USB-powered
device." WakaWaka is an innovative, low-cost solution for people
in the developing world who are living without access to light and
power. Being a "serial entrepreneur," Maurits took an innovative
approach to financing the development of the company. He used
Kickstarter, a global crowdfunding platform for creative ventures,
combined with his personal resources. WakaWaka's business model
is also creative; for every WakaWaka that is purchased, a WakaWaka

Light is donated to a leading aid organization that works with the world's worst humanitarian crises.

WakaWaka is making a significant impact on the lives of people in developing countries living in energy poverty. There are 213,038 WakaWakas, impacting over one million people in 43 countries. This includes survivors of Hurricane Tomas in Haiti, people still struggling with the devastating effects of Typhoon Haiyan in the Philippines and people living in extreme poverty in Mali, Indonesia, and Liberia; 90% of the people in these regions do not have access to electricity. WakaWaka is also helping to bring light to people living in war-torn Syria. There are 10,000 WakaWakas in Syria impacting the lives of 50,000 people and 11,040 tons of CO_2 are displaced every year.

> The WakaWaka is helping us a lot! We don't have to use a kerosene lamp inside the house anymore, which makes us feel healthier and safer. When I have to get up by night to take care of my baby, I can easily turn on the light. And also when we need to go to the toilet outside we use the solar light. On top of these advantages, we save a lot of money! We feel very happy for receiving the light (Indonesian household).

WakaWaka also came to the assistance of the people of Liberia and Sierra Leone by providing light and power to people affected by the Ebola virus. There are 9,831 WakaWakas in Liberia bringing light and power to 49,155 people, which provides 10,764,945 extra hours for work and study every year; 10,853 tons of CO_2 are displaced every year.

> From Jordan to Mali to Guinea-Bissau to Indonesia, we have seen women entrepreneurs—vendors, artisans, healthcare providers and farmers—leverage solar energy as a source of empowerment. Tapping into the abundant power of the sun has increased both entrepreneurship and economic productivity. Women boost household income, providing their families with healthier food, better health care, greater access to education and more savings to get them through less prosperous times (http://us.waka-waka.com).

Meet Maurits Groen

Highest aspiration

The Swahili word *waka waka* means "shine bright." We want everyone to have the opportunity to have a bright life. My ultimate dream is that everyone in the world will have the same quality of life as if they were living in Manhattan: access to light, fridge, TV, computers, the internet, good sanitation, clean water, and good education. We can achieve this in the 21st century because today we already have very efficient, sustainable solutions to achieve this vision. In a couple of years, due to the rapid rate of technological advancements, everyone will be able to afford this quality of life if we can garner the political will to invent clever, innovative financial arrangements that enable people to participate in a higher quality of life. We want to "share the sun," enabled by the WakaWaka solar device to bring light and warmth to everyone. Today, so many people, especially many living in developing countries, are excluded from accessing all this because they cannot afford the one-time, up-front investment of $79 that would enable them to participate in an energy-affluent life. These people end up paying more for less quality in the long run because they can't afford this investment. We want to make it possible for them to make that investment; my task is to think through and implement this goal working across all the sectors, banks, governments, and the private sector.

We are already doing this in some parts of the world and it's expanding. In Africa, for example, 94% of people in rural areas of Africa do not have electricity. Almost everyone now has access to or owns a cell phone or smart phone but the problem is that they need power. They have to walk for miles to another village to pay for charging, then wait for it to be charged before walking all the way home. This is a shame, because in Africa, everywhere, on every single spot on the continent, every day, there is a certainty of sun; so why don't we make it available to people? We have to engage and collaborate with the cell phone companies; it is their core business so it is in their best interest to find ways to help people charge their phones. The same goes for banks. People in Africa primarily use cell phone banking, and in this respect Africa has advanced beyond the US and Europe. So it is in the core interest of banks that people's phones are charged. This applies to governments too. So we are working together with these sectors to enable people to get power. Some African governments are trying to provide power to their people but they are reinventing the wheel. They jump back into the 19th century by building big power plants and hydro-power dams, which cost billions of dollars, take 10 or 15 years to build, and ruin the environment. This is not necessary; if I give people a WakaWaka, they just push the button and they are connected right on the spot— anyone can have power anywhere. WakaWaka is simple and efficient, it uses renewable energy, it's portable, and it's a very convenient way to get power.

My vision is that everyone in the world has the capability to access power. We are the first generation that is aware of the huge global environmental threats that are facing us and, at the same time, we are the first generation that has the knowledge, technology, and the money to solve these problems—so shouldn't we do that? If we do not take on these challenges that are not only big but urgent, we will face very difficult times for civilization at large sooner than we think. We need to work to solve these pressing environmental problems in the next ten years and we need to aim very, very high! If we address these critical issues everyone will benefit and it will elevate everyone's life; for example, it will change the cultural and the social economic condition of women around the world, especially in Africa. Women in Africa are the people that do the work. They are the ones that do the cooking, take care of the water and the fuel and they are raising the new generation. But they are still regarded as second-class citizens. So if they don't have to walk for hours to fetch water and firewood, if they have the money to spend on education instead of on charcoal, they can invest in a one-time efficient device like WakaWaka. As a result, they save time, they save money, they have more income so they can become more independent. This will have significant socioeconomic impact on women and they will be seen in a different way. So it changes their reality; it enables them to spend that time and money educating their children. In one generation the people of Africa could become as educated as the people in the US and Europe. Imagine the benefits of the people of Africa being educated. It would raise the people of Africa's global consciousness about the macro-economic and geopolitical situation. They would start asking very critical questions such as, Why is the wealth of the continent of Africa being extracted? and Why are the profits from those natural resources ending up in the hands of very few, mostly foreigners? If people were educated and had that knowledge they could make massive changes that would lift up the entire population of Africa.

We want to literally enlighten and empower people around the world. This would not just affect poor people, this would change the global socioeconomic, cultural landscape of the world. This off-the-grid solution is like a small bolt yet a powerful core lever. You cannot unknow what you have learned. If people start to realize that we are all connected, if they connect the dots, they will become part of the solution. There are a few on our planet who are holding on to their power out of self-interest, but if we raise the consciousness of billions of people things will change and ultimately all of society will benefit. Solar energy is democratically divided, readily distributed, it is free, and there is certainty that you will have it the next day and for the next 4.5 billion years. There is no energy company that can deliver you safe energy that is free for the next 4.5 billion years. As soon as we realize this, there will be no alternative, we will see the light.

Core values

My core values are **forgiveness**, **equal opportunity**, and **justice**. I think it is very important to look at ourselves in the mirror every once in a while so we don't blame others for things happening in our lives. It is important to ask, How do my actions affect other people and society at large? It is important to try to walk in other people's shoes and to see through other people's eyes; when we do this we tend to forgive more. It is also important that people have equal opportunity, the opportunity to live a good life. I also think that justice is very important. It is simply the Golden Rule, treating people in the way you want to be treated. I try to live my values; there is nothing more enjoyable for me than doing something that I think is good and helping other people. It is much more fun than when you just live for yourself.

Defining moments

My mother's family was and still is made up of farmers who have lived on the same plot of land for at least the past 550 years—talk about sustainable farming! My father's family came from a fishing community so they were regularly confronted with the forces of nature. They were very much dependent on the ocean for food, on the weather, on the technology, on their boats, and on each other for collaboration and cooperation. If they did not work together they would drown; if they did not master their craft, they would starve. They had a very close relationship with the forces of nature. They saw firsthand the beauty and might of nature and the minuteness of self in respect to the whole universe. So my father knew on a very deep level that we are very dependent on the environment, and that became engrained in my DNA.

I have been a serial entrepreneur and champion of sustainability since I was six years old. The first defining moment was when I heard this crazy story that you could reuse scrap paper. I wondered, This is a miracle, how do they make new paper out of old paper, how does the ink disappear? It was magic to me. I thought, we just throw paper away and dump it in landfills and yet we could reuse it, how crazy was that? I just could not understand. So I started collecting old newspapers. I collected hundreds of thousands of kilos and brought them to a recycler. I reasoned that, at least for this paper, no trees will have to be cut. Then I started collecting metals and cloths because they could be recycled and I became a hoarder. For my birthday I received a cart, so I could collect the used materials from all over the neighborhood. That's how I learned about recycling.

Today people are talking about the triple bottom line: economic, social, and environmental sustainability; it has always puzzled me how people could have ever had any other view on this. If you are careful with the way you use energy, how you use materials, how you treat people and your surroundings, if you can reuse stuff, it is more cost-effective and people are happier, healthier, and more productive. That is just logic. I could not understand why the world was going in a different direction. So I just did what I thought was right and what made sense to me.

When I went to university, I studied political science because it integrates, law, sociology, history, communications, international relationships, economics, and philosophy. There are so many people who are experts in their respective fields but are not connected to people in other fields, and that's when things go wrong. So I had to accept that I would never be able to understand everything about one field or everything about every field, but I should try to have an overview and to see the big picture.

The Vietnam War was a defining moment for me. When I stepped back and looked at the big picture, I saw that the most powerful nation on earth was waging a tremendously brutal war against one of the poorest. This was deeply disturbing. The inequality of the treatment of soldiers also affected me; the percentage of Black soldiers killed was much higher than for whites. It seemed to reflect the socioeconomic and racial inequality that existed within the US at that time. Geopolitical issues were also driving the war; the US feared they had to roll back Communism; the whole McCarthyism movement, which was about the political maneuvering of framing innocent people, was still at play. The most powerful driver of the war, however, was the growth and power of the industrial-military complex, which needed war to sell their products and to make money. The reality of the Vietnam War really opened my eyes.

The 1960s civil rights era in America greatly impacted me and helped shape my values and beliefs. I was nine years old in 1963 when President John F. Kennedy was assassinated. I remember picking up a newspaper and reading "Kennedy Shot." Somehow, at nine years old, I knew this would change the world. It was six o'clock on Saturday morning. I ran up the stairs, wrenched open the door of my parents' bedroom, and yelled KENNEDY HAS BEEN KILLED! Five years later, I was watching TV and I saw Sirhan Sirhan kill former attorney general Robert Kennedy; two months after that I saw the report of Martin Luther King's assassination on the balcony of the Lorraine Motel in Memphis, Tennessee; then, two months later the riots broke out at the Democratic convention in Chicago. There were over 100 riots in cities across America in 1968; 39 people died, 34 were Black. I was very affected by what was going on. I read over 100 books during this time to help put things into perspective. All of these events helped inform and shape my world-view. It strongly influenced the development of my core values, especially justice and equal opportunity. I call myself a serial sustainable entrepreneur with these two values in mind.

The WakaWaka journey has been fascinating. It all started with the South Africa World Cup in 2010. The South African government wanted the event to be carbon neutral so they held an international competition to attract the latest innovations in emission reduction. My cofounder, Camille van Gestel, and I entered the competition and won the prize with a highly efficient LED lamp. There was one problem with our solution: many of the people in South Africa lived off the grid so they could not use the lamps, they had no power. I had never visited Africa prior to the competition. This trip opened my eyes to the millions of people who live off the grid. I learned that 1.3 billion people around the world have no easy or convenient access to power. The ramifications are devastating: poor education because children don't have adequate light to study; high crime—women and girls walk home in the dark, therefore the percentage of rapes is high in these communities; ultimately economic opportunities are stifled. The greatest problem is that many people resort to kerosene lamps. These produce toxic fumes, mainly carbon dioxide, which cause respiratory problems; the same effect as smoking two packs of cigarettes a day. A more severe problem with these lamps is that they cause devastating fires. We discovered the horrors of kerosene; I call it the "great kerosene massacre." According to the World Health Organization, 300,000 people die every year and over 6 million are maimed from kerosene fires, mostly women and children, because they are the ones in the house when these kinds of accidents occur. The 6 million people who are maimed are what I call the "walking dead." Who will hire someone who has been disfigured, who will marry them? They are ridiculed for the rest of their lives. People living off the grid in developing countries generally live in shacks built from natural materials such as dried wood and other things that are susceptible to fire. If you spill hot tea you burn yourself but if you spill hot kerosene, you are on fire and in most cases water is not in close proximity, and there are no medical facilities around, so you are done for. If you aren't lucky enough to die you will suffer the rest of your life. This happens around the globe, out of the eyes of the public because there are no media when a shack is burning in a favela or a shanty town; it is not interesting to them. This is happening and we know that it can be prevented. We have the devices that can completely eradicate this horrific situation at an affordable price. I thought we have to develop something to address this injustice. Why haven't the big companies developed a solution to this horrific problem at an affordable price for the people that need it? They have the money and resources, the technology and logistics to develop a solution for such an enormous human need? I always look at things from the positive side but I was mad about this because no other companies were addressing this huge human problem. It is like the diseases that poor people in particular suffer from—there is no money to be made from them. I call this injustice! So we decided to do something about it.

Camille and I discussed how we would start this company. We had all these questions; I had a business, he had a business, so who was going to develop it? How were we going to produce a device? Who was going to sell it? We discussed this for a couple of months and then in July 2011 we said "We can chat about this for ages, let's do something about it." I am a political scientist by training, not a technical person, and I don't know anything about technology; Camille has an MBA; he has some technical insights from working with companies in China but no formal technical expertise. But we knew there were people in the world who did have the expertise and we hired two industrial designers. I said "Guys, we have a big problem, let's solve it together. Let's build a company and let's make a dent on this global problem." Within nine months we were able to produce the most efficient solar light in the world. Two guys with no technical expertise, without any loans from banks or subsidies, took an idea and transformed it into a company that is helping to solve a horrific social problem in the world.

Discoveries and lessons learned

If you give, without the intention of getting something back, you get back more. When the Ebola epidemic broke out, the health workers in Liberia and Sierra Leon asked us to give 7,000 WakaWaka devices. We sent 10,000. It cost us 300,000 euros to produce them. I needed to ship them fast. There was only one airplane going because the disease was so contagious. I called a friend and told him the story and in 50 minutes he gave 65,000 euros, the entire cost of transporting the devices. So if you give you get back, you get back more, but only if you give from the heart. That is a big lesson.

If you trust you are doing the right thing, take a big risk. When I was publishing Al Gore's book, I had to take a second mortgage on my house. Why would he say yes to me? Why would he come the Netherlands? But I trusted I was doing the right thing. I have taken many big risks and they have always worked out so far.

You can never dream too big! We are going to solve the energy poverty problem before I retire; if it can be solved, it will be solved.

Trust people. Give people a lot of freedom to develop themselves and to make mistakes. I want to have the freedom to make mistakes and to learn from them. I have a lot of ideas, crazy ideas, so I need the space to explore them, make mistakes, and to learn from them so I can do better the next time. I should trust people to do the same.

Abolish "if" and "should." In this company we abolish these two words and we replace them with "will" and "when." If it is necessary, it will happen and it is up to us; so how are we going to do it, and how fast will it take? That is our state of mind.

You degrade people if you just give them things. People are not lazy or bad, they are just in a situation. Was it my personal achievement that I was born in a rich country? I admire people trying to sell candy on the corner or working on the docks. When you give people things you are acting superior; it suggests, "I am giving you this from my superior position." So just make it affordable within the context of their economy; what is achievable in Sierra Leone is different from what is achievable in Amsterdam. So our business model is to make things affordable, in relative terms. In Haiti, we donated WakaWakas to the NGOs and in return they teach children. They provide a service so in effect they pay for it with service to the community.

This is the richest generation that ever lived on the face of this earth. I am living in the fifth richest country in the world. I have the obligation, the responsibility, and the possibility to do something; to solve these big social and environmental problems. A lot of people hold on to their money; they are afraid. I pity them because they are incarcerated in their own mental construction.

What I learned from Maurits Groen

Maurits' values and character were shaped by the big global events that happened during his life. Many times we are told that the things that matter to us most are those we tend to in our personal life, not matters for business or work. Maurits' passion for social justice in the world has become his business.

WakaWaka has become a highly successful suite of innovative products that have received a great deal of recognition in the market place, and they have brought light and warmth to hundreds of thousands of people living in energy poverty. Maurits is proving that innovating for the greater good makes good businesses sense.

Jérôme Michaud-Larivière, founder, President, and CEO, NewWind

4
NewWind and the WindTree: a writer, a poet, and a wind tree

> When I created NewWind in 2011, the first design principle was to create a wind power device that had an organic form and was as pleasant as possible. Then very quickly we realized that beyond the form, we were able to produce something else: we could create a design that people were proud of and that engendered positive emotions. We could make a small but vital contribution to the emergence of sensitive cities. The strong support that we receive every day from people demonstrates that consumers are willing to change the current energy model. We are pleased to support this movement and thus help everyone to find a calmer place in the world (Jérôme Michaud-Larivière, innovator and CEO, NewWind R&D).

Over the past five years I have become acutely aware of the climate change crisis and the urgent need for clean, renewable energy. My participation as an advisory board member of the Fowler Center for Business as an Agent of World Benefit has heightened my awareness of the current environmental crisis. Like many people today, I feel a sense of urgency to do whatever I can to help mitigate the harm we have caused to the environment and to help renew our planet. One way I hope I am helping is by shining a light on fascinating innovators such as Jérôme Michaud-Larivière, founder and CEO of New Wind. Jérôme believes that form and function are both critical requirements for good design. It is critical that the new solutions help us to reverse the mounting environmental threats; it is also important that these new technologies contribute to the health and well-being of people, animals, and the planet. The great American designer Charles Eames called designs that both solve a problem and nurture the human spirit "good goods."

On my quest to find people innovating for the greater good, I came across a small article in *Inhabit.com*, a newsletter described as an "online guide to the best green design ideas, innovations and inspiration to build a cleaner, brighter, and better future." The title of the article was "New Silent Wind Tree turbines make energy beautiful," and it pictured Jérôme's Wind Tree. At first glance it looked like a sculpture adorning an office building. So I was very curious when I discovered it was a wind turbine. I am a big proponent of clean renewable energy solutions, but the huge wind turbines I see in fields along the highway are very imposing. Of course I will take them over any of the fossil-based energy sources, but to be honest, their size, sound, and structure are somewhat intimidating.

My curiosity led me to Paris to meet the genius who had the insight and sensitivity to invent a solution to the energy crisis whose design is in harmony with people and nature. I walked into an R&D studio in the 7th District of Paris that was abuzz with young engineers busy transforming Jérôme's vision into reality. Jérôme showed me a prototype and indeed it was beautiful. The Arbre à Vent® (Wind Tree) stands 26 feet (9 m) tall, the size of an average tree, and has 54 artificial leaves (L'Aeroleaf®). The leaves are the color of nature in early spring, and though they are larger that most tree leaves, they are elegantly designed. They generate electricity from the slightest breeze and they move gracefully and silently. The Wind Tree is beautiful and safe for people and animals, and it complements the surrounding environment. This graceful Wind Tree can supply enough energy for 15 street lights or electrical independence for a typical household for a year. Imagine the possibilities!

Jérôme's innovative Wind Tree was introduced to the world in Europe in 2015. It was displayed at the historic United Nations Climate Change Conference held in Paris, France (see Fig. 4.1). The response from people, communities, and businesses has been

FIGURE 4.1   The Wind Tree on display at the UN Climate Change Conference, Paris, 2015

outstanding. People appreciate the Wind Tree's beauty; its influence with the environment, both with communities and with the natural environment; its simplicity: you just plug in in and it's ready to go; and its durability: it has a lifespan of 20 years. People especially appreciate that it is a powerful solution to the pressing energy crisis facing humanity. "The Wind Tree epitomizes the current move towards decentralized energy production solutions, low-carbon and proximity. And besides, when it's as beautiful as the Wind Tree, it's even better" (Gérard Mestrallet, Chairman and former CEO, Engie).

Meet Jérôme Michaud-Larivière

Jérôme's vision

I'm a modest person and I see myself as a citizen of society; however, I have always believed that if one day I could do something useful for society, my life would then be complete. I am not an engineer, I am a

FIGURE 4.2   Imagining Wind Trees along the banks of the River Seine

poet and a writer, but I believe we need to redesign cities for the future; we need smart, green cities but I wanted to play with the concepts of proximity and beauty in the design of smart cities. I believe it is possible to design what I call sensitive cities. These are cities that are graceful and elegant and enable us to live in harmony with nature and with each other.

My vision is to have Wind Trees everywhere, but especially in urban areas; 75% of people will live in cities by the year 2050. The need for green electricity will grow exponentially because nearly everyone is convinced that fossil-based energy is no longer viable in the long term. We need to find green energy solutions that are beautifully designed, quiet, discreet, not imposing, in sync with nature and efficient, and all at an affordable price.

My deep desire is that these new forms of energy go far beyond beauty and good design. We need to produce energy in proximity to the consumer to enable people to generate their own electricity with at least two advantages. First, it must stir our emotions. We want solutions that invoke pride in people; we have forgotten about "pride" in many of our energy solutions. Second, it must be affordable. There is a lot of poverty in the world and electricity is expensive. There is already considerable inequality in our world—social inequality and especially energy inequality. Our green energy solutions must not increase that division. When you look at the Wind Tree producing energy it is very sweet; it requires only a subtle breeze and it is absolutely quiet, the birds are singing, so it not only kind to humans, it is nurturing to the environment.

The biomimetic-inspired design is ideal in all types of landscapes, whether urban or rural. All the technology is invisible; the cable and generator are integrated into the branches and trunk. Each leaf of the tree produces electricity from the slightest breath of air from any direction. The tree adds an aesthetic and emotional value to cityscapes (see Fig. 4.2). It is a simple "plug and play" system and is low voltage and safe. It can be placed close to buildings; it doesn't interfere with existing electrical lines and in most places does not require special permits. The Wind Tree is durable, designed to withstand storms, and expected to last 20 years.

Core values

Freedom, **creativity**, and **innovation** are important to me. I am looking for harmony, but it is very difficult to create harmony when you innovate. To create an innovation runs counter to harmony because the process of innovating is a struggle. To innovate you have to be a rebel. It is very difficult because a new idea is always met with inertia; inertia of knowledge and disbelief that it is possible to transform that new idea into reality. It is met with resistance because the original idea, the status quo, is firmly planted in people's minds. It is met with silence and viewed with skepticism. It is often met with mockery at the beginning; they laughed at me when I talked about the Wind Tree. People thought it was impossible to make and because I was not an engineer, they thought it was a fantasy. Scientists are limited by their knowledge and it is hard for them to get out of the box to see a new way because they are firmly rooted in current knowledge and new ideas are viewed as disruptive. They are very clever builders but it is difficult for them to access their imagination. I am a writer; creativity is my gift and therefore I am free, I can get out of the box, I can imagine a whole new approach.

I strongly believe there should be a link, a connection, between the consumer and the means of production to bring warmth and light into homes. That is very important to me. My secret ambition, my highest aspiration, is to bring light and warmth into every home on the planet. So you can imagine when I talk like this people look at me as though I am crazy. I'm not crazy, the design of our cities should be a reflection of the best of who we are; our personalities, our kindness, our smiles. To bring light and warmth into homes, that is my baseline mission.

Defining moments

I am a poet and a writer but I have a scientific spirit. Science is in my DNA because I was raised in a scientific environment. I am the only one in my family who is not an engineer, I am the outlier. I come from a family of well-known engineers in France. Every member of my family has been dedicated to the development of cities, trains, planes, railroad stations and bridges. I was drawn to literature but I nursed from the bottle of science, it is in my body and in my intuition.

For years I was a writer for some popular TV series here in France: *Soeur Thérèse.com*, *Diane, femme flic* and *Camping Paradis*. Every day I would create a scene for the show and then forget it and start all over again the next day. When I turned 50 I decided it was important to do something meaningful and more useful for society. I was thinking about the energy problem, pollution on one side and the energy crisis on the other. We have to find a way to change the economic model that prevails today. I believe that energy sources and consumer needs should be in close proximity and aesthetically pleasing. It also needs to be efficient and able to transform the look of the city. I had all these questions in my head.

In 2010 while still grappling with these questions, I was writing a new novel. I put all my questions and interest in the energy crises into the plot of the book. The main character was a doctor, a very important figure in the field of energy. I wanted him to have a big idea, an invention, something that would make a significant impact on the story. But I was stuck on page 40; I needed to find an idea. So I went for a walk. It was a sunny day and there was no discernable breeze. As I looked at the trees, I noticed that the leaves were trembling; I was fascinated, and the idea of the scientist in my novel inventing a Wind Tree popped in my head.

I went to my room and finished the scene. I did some research on the internet to convince the reader that the doctor was legitimate. The book was published, and eight or nine months later I was meeting with my publisher and he congratulated me on the success of my book. Then he asked enthusiastically, "Oh, by the way, where can I buy that Wind Tree? I want one for my country house." I told him the Wind Tree doesn't exist: it was just in my imagination; I invented it for the novel. He wasn't happy about that. He said, "That's a shame. It should exist." If I had not had that encounter with my publisher, it is possible that the Wind Tree would have never happened. That discussion was the catalyst for creating a Wind Tree that brings warmth and light to people; produces clean sustainable energy in close proximity to the people; is aesthetically pleasing and evokes pride and a sense of wellbeing; is affordable; and is harmonious with the surrounding environment and nature.

The Wind Tree was still just a good idea. We worked through the technical development challenges, but the core solutions came from my intuition. I believe once you open up your imagination, the right solutions and opportunities can suddenly present themselves. The timing was also right. France had just entered a phase in which the government had begun to generously subsidize innovative startups with grants, low rents, and other enabling services to help them flourish, especially those innovations that benefit society.

How far we have come

We officially launched the Wind Tree in 2011 in France, Belgium, Switzerland, and Germany. Our first project was the Piguet Galland Bank, a private bank based in Switzerland.

We are happy and proud to be among the first to erect this magnificent Wind Tree, which is as much a work of art as it is an innovation in sustainable development. We were particularly sensitive to the environmental approach of Jérôme Michaud-Larivière. We hope that this initiative will be followed by many others and that beyond this first Wind Tree a whole forest lies! (Olivier Calloud, Chief Executive Officer, Banque Piguet Galland).

We have several exciting projects in development, including the Astainable project, which aims to develop Astana, the capital of Kazakhstan, into a smart sustainable city. The Wind Tree is one of the solutions to help them realize their vision. Valerie David, Director Sustainable Development for Eiffage, one of the partners in the project, says: "We found in New Wind an ambitious start-up that as part of the renewable energy sector, has been able to design an attractive product, that combines the ecological relevance and an attractive design."

Obstacles and challenges

When I first talked about the idea, people thought I was crazy. They thought I was a dreamer and they laughed. So the principal difficulty was to convince people that the idea was not so poetic that it could not actually be produced or be practically useful. It is sometimes difficult for engineers to imagine transforming a dream into reality and I had to convince my team of engineers and developers that we could do it. I had to convince them to take the leap into the unknown. It takes a lot of time and effort to transform a creative idea into a prototype.

Personal impact

Having a big, bold vision that can change the world is inspiring and fulfilling. It gives me a purpose much greater than myself and I have been dedicated to that vision. I invested £200,000 in the Wind Tree, thanks to my TV show. The Wind Tree journey has kept me young and relevant and it uplifts my spirits.

What I learned from Jérôme Michaud-Larivière

In the midst of all the chaos in our world, this interview, like every story in this book, gave me hope. It expanded my vision of what is possible. I now envision Wind Trees lining the city streets of Tokyo and Jakarta, Delhi and Shanghai, Mexico City and New York City. I can imagine a Wind Tree in every backyard in neighborhoods from Detroit to San Francisco to Atlanta. I dream of Wind Trees bringing energy to people in the villages and communities of Rwanda and the favelas in Rio de Janeiro.

Imagine the Wind Tree bringing relief to the overstressed and deteriorating US electrical grid, giving cities and the country the opportunity to repair and renew their aging electrical systems. Imagine families having electrical independence and leveraging their $23,000 investment over a period of 20 years.

I am an insatiable learner, so my 20-year quest to shine a light on DreamMakers, has taken me on a fascinating voyage of inquiry and discovery, which has brought me an abundance of aha! moments. This encounter with Jérôme and his Wind Tree was one of those moments that have led me to dream big.

The possibilities for the Wind Tree are numerous and the impact on people and society could be life-changing. The Wind Tree could help to create a world where **people can thrive, businesses can prosper and the planet can flourish.**

Menlo Innovations cofounders
From left: Robert Simms (CFO), Richard Sheridan (CEO and chief storyteller),
and James Goebel (COO, Chief Architect)

5
Menlo Innovations: joy at work

Richard Sheridan, cofounder of Menlo Innovations so passionately believes that "joy" is a powerful value proposition that he wrote the book, *Joy, Inc.: How We Built a Workplace People Love.*[1] I consider myself a tenacious activist *for* people. For as long as I can remember I have been fighting for human rights, and one human right I believe in is that people should be able to bring their whole self to work. Asking people to compartmentalize their personality and emotions has to be harmful to people's health and well-being. It also stifles creativity and productivity. So I was elated when I ran across *Joy, Inc.* I had to see for myself if this place was authentic or a public relations ploy, and so I went to Ann Arbor, Michigan, to meet with Rich, the cofounder, CEO and Chief Storyteller.

I got there early and a young man greeted me with a warm smile and invited me to look around while Rich finished up a meeting, then he left and I was free to roam. I loved the feel of the place. It was a completely open office design, full of people huddled in teams around computers, and small crowds standing around whiteboards. Yes, you could feel the joy, but the joy seemed to come from the focus they had on their projects; you could feel that people were building something they cared about—together. Then out walked this 6 ft 5 in man beaming with pride and smiling from ear-to-ear.

1   Sheridan, R. (2013). *Joy, Inc.: How We Built a Workplace People Love.* New York: Portfolio/Penguin.

Menlo Way

Innovative practices at Menlo Innovations

- Pairing
- High Tech Anthropology
- open and collaborative workspace
- high speed voice technology
- *daily stand up*
- *40 hour work weeks*
- pets and babies at work
- making mistakes faster

- *doing the simplest thing that could possibly work*
- origami project mgmt
- *work authorization boards; story cards, yarn, and stickers*
- estimation without fear
- *integrated quality advocacy*
- *test-driven development*

FIGURE 5.1   The Menlo Way

For the next two hours I was swept up in the Menlo story and the personal journey that led Rich to pursue this radical culture of joy in the workplace.

Menlo Innovations, founded in 2001, is a custom software design company, or as Rich describes it, "If you have the house of your dreams in mind, you would want to find an architectural firm, a design firm, and a build firm to bring it to life. We do the same thing for software." Their mission is "to end human suffering in the world as it relates to technology"™ and their mission truly does start with themselves. They have developed a unique organizational culture that is genuinely rooted in the Business Value of Joy™. They are so committed to this way of being and working that part of their mission is to spread the word. They give tours, hold workshops, give keynote presentations at conferences and, of course, Rich wrote the book. To Rich, joy means far more than happy: "Joy is a word that carries the connotation of love, happiness, health, purpose, and values."

The Menlo culture, work systems and processes are completely aligned with Menlo's mission and beliefs. Its culture is open, transparent, collaborative, relational, and non-hierarchical, and there is a spirit of invention that is safe from fear. I saw a poster on the wall that read: "Make Mistakes Faster."

Menlo's workspace also reflects its culture and values. Patterned after Menlo Park, Thomas Edison's "invention factory" in New Jersey, the Menlo Software Factory is wide open, adaptable, and built for collaboration and teamwork—superstars need not apply.

> At Menlo, we work in close collaboration. Therefore, our first interviewing im perative is: "Do you have good kindergarten skills?" Are you respectful? Do you play well with others? Do you share? During what we call our "Extreme Interview," we will mention good kindergarten skills several times, since it's tantamount to our joyful culture that you play well with others. This is not a theoretical or rhetorical concept. Given we work in pairs all day long, this is crucial (Richard Sheridan, CEO, Menlo Innovations).

> My sister saves babies for a living. I am not that kind of hero. But, I do help to "end human suffering as it relates to technology." As a High-Tech Anthropologist, I get to be part of designing tools that help cure cancer, help people manage diabetes, and help people apply to programs that can save them from foreclosure. These types of projects give me great personal satisfaction in making a difference in the world (Michelle Pomorski, High Tech Anthropologist® Menlo Innovations).

Meet Richard Sheridan

Highest aspirations

My highest aspiration is to bring joy into the workplace. Our definition of joy is the interaction that results in people saying "I love that product." It is when the work of our hearts, hands, and minds goes out into the world and delights the people it's intended to serve. Our mission is "to end human suffering in the world as it relates to technology," and there are three kinds of suffering. The first kind of suffering we wish to address is that of the product manager, the person who is in charge of getting the product built and out into the marketplace. That person wants to build something, spends money, and then it fails; now they can't steer the project to a successful conclusion. The software team they hired explains why it's not ready, talking in mumbo jumbo, techno-geek language with three-letter acronyms and waving their hands, telling the product manager "it's done but it's not finished" or "it's finished but it's not ready." That product manager doesn't understand a word they are saying. They are praying every night that the software will deliver what was promised. The number of times that projects fail in our industry is astronomical. You can't imagine how many people show up at Menlo's doorstep who have spent millions and millions of dollars with nothing to show for it. That's the first kind of suffering we are trying to end. We can put that product manager in the driver's seat with a steering wheel that they understand how to use and they can drive their project to conclusion.

The second kind of suffering we are trying to end is that of the people who build the software. There is nothing more discouraging than to work for years on something, most often with a huge amount of overtime, then when the thing is supposed to launch, it can't get out the door. Let's look at one of our more salient examples: Healthcare.gov. President Obama came before the nation two days before the launch date and announced that the team in charge had told him the website would be ready on schedule. On the launch date, millions of people could not get onto the website. Two days later, he had to go back to the nation after learning of numerous bugs and glitches, missed schedules, and gaping security holes, and he had to apologize. The President of the United States had to apologize to the nation for the failed software project! Congressional hearings reveal that when the website went live, 40% of the project had not even begun. President Obama must have been wondering what happened two days before the launch that made everybody say it was okay? Then the president told the nation not to worry, they have people working 24/7 to bring the website back on line. Quite frankly, when he made that statement, that's when I began to worry because tired programmers make poor software and there is no chance to work with pride under those circumstances. When you say we have a program team working 24/7, that is not three shifts, that's the same people working round the clock and being away from their families, so there is a lot of suffering going on there. Can you imagine what it felt like being a part of the team that developed the software?

The last kind of suffering is inflicted on the user, let's call him Brad. He thinks, what are they doing? Did they ever talk to the people who have

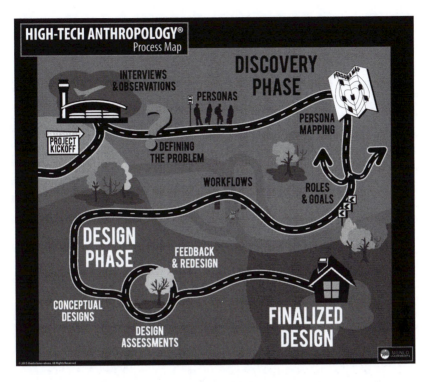

FIGURE 5.2   High-Tech Anthropology® process map

to use the software? This is where our High-Tech Anthropology process comes into play.

This process starts with the end-user, the customer. The High-Tech Anthropology team (we call them HTAs) study the end-user. They learn about the user's workflow, their habits and their goals as human beings. They bring all that information back to the design sessions. Like traditional anthropologists, they spend a great deal of the time out in the world studying people in their native environment. Most software projects don't have this stage, so what happens is that really smart technical people sit in a room and believe they know how the customer works; but they don't. They build the software, it goes through the entire process to the customer, and it is not what the customer needs. At Menlo, the HTAs work with everyone in the process, throughout the process, to make sure the software is meeting the customer's needs.

In the Healthcare.gov example, I can imagine what happened. The president's chief information officer (CIO) spends tens of millions of dollars hiring some big software company. As the project moves forward, all of the information that is going back to her has a "green light," everything is good, we are right on target. How would she know if that information is correct because there is no way for her to peek into the process to check progress? So all she can go by is the status reports. Healthcare.gov is the president's signature program, so I imagine that every once in a while she sits down with the president to give him a progress report. She tells him everything is fine and he goes before the nation and says, "we are good to go." The American people were so hopeful that they would finally be able to have healthcare coverage for their families. They were feeling relieved that if anything happened to their loved ones, they would have health insurance. They went to their computers, tried to sign into the healthcare.gov website, and they just got the spinning dial. They waited and they waited and nothing happened, the whole thing fell apart. So millions of people were very frustrated; the president had been talking about this for six years, Hillary Clinton had been working on this in the 1990s, so millions of Americans were very disappointed. The president was frustrated, millions of dollars were basically thrown away, the CIO was fired, the development firm was fired … there was a whole lot of suffering as a result. Here is the interesting thing; this is what was so confounding, I bet everyone who worked on the project, everyone who was involved, was incredibly well intentioned; it was the system that failed everyone.

Menlo has created a different system, one that takes care of all of the people in the process. In order to do that we had to change the whole system, we changed everything! This is the hard part; this is why it is hard being us. We changed everything, including something as simple as having two people at every computer. Some people said that seems really expensive; we say, compared to what? We call this **pairing** (Fig. 5.3). The miraculous thing is that this is an incredibly simple idea, but simple is often hard. A man called Fred Brooks wrote a book about 30 years ago called *The Mythical Man-Month*.[2] Fred was a well-known software guy. He

2   Brooks, F. (1975). *The Mythical Man-Month*. Reading, MA: Addison-Wesley.

FIGURE 5.3   Pairing is the foundation of Menlo's work style

looked at all the chaos that was in this industry. When a project is late a natural response from management is to put more people on it. Brooks said, "Adding manpower to a late software project makes it later." Today, that concept is called Brooks' law. This is an accepted belief and when you have a "law" in your industry "it shall not be broken." At Menlo, we break Brooks' law with impunity.

I want to show you the secret to **pairing**. It is like magic and I will tell you how it works; I'm a magician that reveals his secrets. These four people are assigned to the Argos project for the week, two at each computer. Next week, each of them will be switched to another project, so with four people we get three different pairings. If one of them takes a vacation, we grab another person to fill out the team. So what are we doing? What is happening is that there is information being shared between all the team members, they are talking things through, and they are building mental models in their heads—*together*. When people switch teams they naturally ask questions and their teammate has to explain and bring the new member up to date. So the information exchange is constantly happening. Now let's say the customer comes in with a new deadline; they need the software sooner. Our response is, cool, you need to get twice as much done, so we are going to add four more people to this project. We pair each of them with an existing team member, we add two more computers and put them all together in close proximity. So one half of each pair is always experienced in the project. After four weeks of this we have eight people experienced in the project. Now if the customer comes back and says we need to go even faster, we add even more people and more computers, still pairing two people per computer. Menlonians don't get frustrated that they are not coming up with the right solution because they have someone right next to them to support them, and if one pair can't figure it out, they have other pairs next to them they can turn to. So the team just expands—more pairs might join them or if they are really stuck they just run up to the white board and call a bigger meeting. We have a lot of flexibility built into the process.

Our industry can't even fathom what I have just described. It results in everyone having a 40-hour work week; we never work on weekends and we never deny a vacation request; if we need more done we add more people. Menlonians are not burned out, they are not going home exhausted and they are not feeling isolated and lonely. In that simple way of working, we have created a humanly sustainable system to get work done. Now Menlonians have a chance to work with pride. That is what we call joy. People ask us: "Are you really playful at work?" Yes, there has to be some fun in the room, but there are no ping-pong tables here, nothing like that. People here work incredibly hard pursuing something that is bigger than themselves; ending human suffering in our industry and delighting the end-user.

We orient our customers to this process so they can understand its value. That's why I wrote the book, *Joy Inc.* and that's why we conduct Joy, Inc. Customer Tours. If the customers don't understand why we work like this, the process just looks expensive; I say it *looks* expensive, but compared to what? When people could not signup for Healthcare.gov because the site did not work and the president had to fire the CIO, that was a multi-hundred-million-dollar error. I can assure you we would have not used several hundred million dollars here to build Healthcare.com.

I am pleased to report that Brooks' law can be broken and we have the data to show that by using the Menlo Way we outperform the industry.

I am living my life's vision at Menlo and that vision is a gift. When I was 20 and a student at the University of Michigan, I was out walking down State Street thinking about my future and I perfectly imagined Menlo, just as it is today—open space, and a highly collaborative team. It could not have been a more perfect imagine. I never thought about it again until about six years into Menlo. I walked into Menlo one day and it was like a little jack-in-the-box jumped out smiling and said "Congratulations, you accomplished the dream of your 20-year-old self." I thought how could this happen, how could my vision so perfectly manifest? This was the gift I was given when I was 20 and it lay there under the tree until almost 30 years later when I opened it.

Defining moments

I have actually thought a lot about this, because people often ask me, where does the joy come from for you? Even the Menlo team jokes "oh, the Chief Optimist." I had parents who loved me very dearly. I was blessed because as parents they were about as perfect as you could get. As husband and wife they were average, they loved each other, but they loved us more. We grew up in a tiny tract home in Macomb County, Michigan, and I remember in the 1960s when we would go out for a family movie, which was a big treat. My dad would have us play this game where we would search in the chair cushions for coins. I remember that as just being fun. Now I look back on it, if we had not actually found a few quarters that had fallen out of my dad's pockets, maybe we couldn't have afforded to go to the movies. I think there were many times when my mom and dad lived paycheck to paycheck, but we never knew it. That never spilled out to us kids because we had an abundance of love in our household and that is a remarkable advantage. My mom's favorite movie was *Camelot* and her favorite line was from the song "How to Handle a Woman." The line was "love her, simply love her, just love her." That was my mom. My dad was the same, in his own way.

Let me give you one incident that was definitely a defining moment in my life; it happened when I was ten years old. I have always been a builder. In my mind engineers are builders, we make things out of stuff, this is the heart of engineers; we love to build things. My parents had bought what in the 1960s would be the equivalent of today's Ikea shelving unit. It was in a box in the garage. My mom was so excited she was going to have this beautiful new shelving unit in the living room; I knew she could picture it in her mind. My parents went out to dinner and a movie one night and I was left on my own so I decided to build her shelving unit. So I went out to the garage, opened up the box and I put it together—50 pieces of wood and 200 little nuts, bolts, and screws—using a 50-page booklet. I put this whole thing together and it was huge, about 6 feet tall and 8 feet across. I was so excited to show it to them. And then I realized I had built it in the garage. I was so determined that I inched that shelving unit out of the garage, down the sidewalk, into the house, past the family room, past the kitchen, right into the living room. I set up all the books, put the stereo on it, and put a record on. When my mom walked in she was so delighted that she cried. In that moment so much pride swelled up in me. To me, that right there is the definition of joy! Because what happened was the work of my hands, my mind, and my heart, and it brought delight to the person it was intended to serve. It was a struggle to build and move that unit but I didn't care; what mattered to me was that moment I witnessed my mother's reaction. When I think of what we are doing here at Menlo, that's it. I want to give my team that feeling I had when my mother saw the shelving unit. I want them to know what it feels like when people say, I love what you did, you guys are amazing; we get that here and we get it regularly. That's Joy, Inc. Joy is designing and building something that actually sees the light of day, is used with delight and widely adopted by the people for whom it was intended. I built that unit because I loved my parents, and I love these people, the Menlonians.

Another thing that influenced my life was Greenfield Village, the Henry Ford American History museum and the home of Thomas Edison's Menlo Park laboratory. When you grow up in southeast Michigan as a kid you go to Greenfield Village. Whenever I walked into Thomas Edison's Menlo Park lab, I got goose bumps; I don't know why but it had an effect on me. I was greatly influenced by Edison's Menlo Park Experience. According to Bill Pretzer in *Working at Inventing: Thomas A. Edison and the Menlo Park Experience*,[3] Ford's goal was "to create a museum that would not only record the past but would shape the future as well." Henry Ford's vision was "to use the past to encourage visitors, especially the young, to aspire to great achievements of their own." I owe my personal story to Henry Ford; his vision worked for me.

The critical moment that caused Menlo to exist was the fight I had with my boss Bob Nero at Interface. When he said, Rich I want you to be the Vice President of R&D for this public company, I said no and he got angry and threw me out of his office. I went home that night and reflected on what I wanted to accomplish in my life. Why had I gotten into this profession in the first place? I thought through everything and realized, this is your moment! This is what you have been waiting for, seize the day! I went back the next day and told him "Bob, I'll do it, on one condition—you provide me with the support so that I can build the best software team this town has ever seen." He supported me. Menlo would not exist were it not for that man's influence on me; he was my Max De Pree. He is one of my best friends today; we love each other. He is a great man and was the perfect guy at the perfect time for me, and it could not have lined up better.

Core values: what matters most in life

Relationships are important to me. Have you ever read a great book by Michael Ray called *The Highest Goal?*[4] He is a professor at Stanford Business School. In that book he goes through an exercise that identifies those moments that meant more to you than anything else. When you put yourself in that frame of mind it's remarkable how those moments come flooding back. It's as if there is a special little box in your brain where all of your best life experiences have been stored away; we don't think about them often but when we are asked to recall them they just

3   Prenzer, W.F. (1989). *Working at Inventing: Thomas A. Edison and the Menlo Park Experience*. Dearborn, MI: Henry Ford Museum and Greenfield Village.

4   Ray, M. (2004). *The Highest Goal: The Secret That Sustains You in Every Moment*. Oakland, CA: Berrett-Koehler.

start flowing out. Then he asked the question "Why is that important to you?" and if you keep asking that question you will ultimately get it down to one word. The word that I got to was "relationship." Why did building that shelving unit for my parents delight me? It was because I was in a great relationship with them. James Goebel, my cofounder, and I have a great relationship. My wife works here at Menlo and we have a great relationship. The way we work at Menlo is all about relationships, the way we work together and with our clients. The Menlo system here is designed around relationships. For me being in strong relationships is core, it's fundamental. That's my heart.

Bringing joy by ending human suffering in technology is our mission and what matters to us most. One of my highest moments here at Menlo was when our client shipped the first flow cytometer (a blood research device for which we developed the software) in February 2008. That was a very special day because we worked for three and a half years to make it happen. This device revolutionized the market for cancer research. When the first unit shipped, Leo, the customer support lead, called the customer and told them it would be there the next day. He asked the customer to call him as soon as it arrived. Leo checked the FedEx tracking and saw that someone signed for it at 8:45 a.m. Leo camped out by the telephone and waited for the customer to call; it got to be noon and still no phone call. Then the next day goes by, no phone call, and now Leo was despondent. Finally, he called the customer and asked, "Did you get the box ok?" The customer said "Oh yes, we got the unit yesterday morning." Leo said, "Why didn't you call me?" The customer responded, "Oh we just started using it; we have been doing research on it for two days now." You see, if you can ship a complex piece of medical research hardware and software with no user manual, no help desk, no training classes, and no support calls, that's lower cost at a higher price. They simply unpacked it and started using it that same day. When we built the Menlo Way system we believed that the system would work but we really did not know because it was a dream, a vision; and then that happens. Just like that, you know it works! We wanted to end the customer's suffering and we did it. That was impactful. The team was very, very proud!

Greatest obstacles

It's funny, kind of like raising children; if people were to ask me what was the hardest thing about raising my daughter, it's hard to remember. Yes, there were sleepless nights, or we worried about this thing or that thing, you think about of all those things, but were they obstacles? No it's just what happens. A tree falls down you just crawl over it. You fall down and hurt your head, you decide to wear a hard hat the next time. There were lots of things we had to fight through but to me that's just life and they were informative to our journey.

Greatest lessons

My father taught me a very powerful lesson. I was a Boy Scout, my father was the scout master and he pushed me to become an Eagle Scout (the highest achievement level of the Scouts in the US). I did not want to do it. I was 16 years old and being a Boy Scout was starting to feel a little silly. I felt I was outgrowing that phase of my life. My father said to me, "Don't you dare stop early—you will regret it the rest of your life if you do." I am glad I listened to him.

Another important lesson that I learned and live by is, "Leave the campsite better than you found it." My campsite is planet earth. I need to have lived a life that made a difference.

What I learned from Rich Sheridan

Who knew that joy could be a powerful business proposition? And that people do not have to compartmentalize themselves when they walk into the door of their workplace. Rich and his cofounders have demonstrated that joy can be a powerful business strategy that generates commitment, innovation, and high-quality results. It was a joy to be at Menlo; I felt it, I sensed it in the people that worked there, and it showed in their products and their processes. Rich was overflowing with joy—it was contagious. Business leaders have a great deal to learn from this approach to doing business.

Chuck Fowler, Chairman, and retired CEO of Fairmount Santrol

6
Fairmount Santrol: boldly different

 *FairmountSantrol*

I first met Chuck Fowler in 2011 when I joined the advisory board of the Fowler Center for Business as an Agent of World Benefit. My first impression of Chuck has not wavered over the six years I have worked with him. He is a good soul, an honest person who leads with kindness. He authentically cares about people and he is secure enough to show it. I have met hundreds of CEOs in my 30 years working with corporate executives. Chuck's personality and sensibilities and his approach to leadership are rare in the C-suites of corporate America.

Chuck is deeply committed to a flourishing future for people and the planet. This is not a frivolous dream for him; it is a compelling vision that he actively works to help realize. In an era when many CEOs have a single aim to make, protect and shield their money, Chuck and his wife, Char, endowed $7.5 million to establish the Fowler Center for Business as an Agent of World Benefit at the Weatherhead School of Management at Case Western Reserve University. It was in 2007 when they made this endowment to broaden and accelerate the vision of a world where **people can thrive, business can prosper and the planet can flourish**. David Cooperrider, who had worked with Chuck and Fairmount Santrol to help create this vision, was appointed director of the Center. The Fowler Center has been discussed in detail in Chapter 2.

Chuck is the founder, Chairman and retired CEO of Ohio-based Fairmount Santrol, the third largest producer of industrial sand in the United States. It is a billion-dollar global corporation with 26

2014 FAIRMOUNT FAMILY SUMMIT

UNITED + EMPOWERED

FIGURE 6.1   The landmark Appreciative Inquiry Summit in 2014 led to a sustainable vision for the future of Fairmont Santrol

production facilities and 50 distribution locations throughout North America, Europe and Asia. It is a vision-led and values-based company with approximately 1,000 "Family Members," a term the employees collectively decided to call themselves.

> Fairmount Santrol is Boldly Different in our strong commitment to all three pillars of sustainable development (SD): People, Planet, and Prosperity. By actively living our motto and action orientation of "Do Good. Do Well". ... Our Family Members are deeply engaged in our commitment to exceed all expectations while fulfilling our economic, social, and

FIGURE 6.2   Appreciative Inquiry Summit, 2014: Day Of Caring

environmental responsibilities (Jenniffer Deckard, President and Chief Executive Officer, Fairmount Santrol *Social Responsibility Report*, 2014).

Fairmount Santrol has co-created a sustainable culture that has earned numerous regional and national awards for their sustainable business practices, including the U.S. Chamber of Commerce Business Civic Leadership Center and Corporate Stewardship Award, and the Ford Motor Co. World Excellence Award for Corporate Social Responsibility.

The sustainable development of **people, planet, and prosperity** is the way Fairmount Santrol conducts business; it is a way of life for them. Every three years, since 2005, the company brings half of its Family Members, customers and key stakeholders together for three days, to help shape the future of the company. This company development process is facilitated by the Weatherhead School professors David Cooperrider and Ron Fry, the cofounders of Appreciative Inquiry (AI), a powerful, highly collaborative, organizational development methodology used to inspire positive change by building on an organization's

FIGURE 6.3 Fairmount Santrol's family members planted 132,000 trees in 2015

Source: Fairmount Santrol *Corporate Resonsibility Report*, 2015.

strengths. In 2014, the company held a landmark AI Summit where Family Members and 60 external stakeholders came together to co-create their vision for a sustainable future and agreed on the steps to get there (Fig. 6.1). They developed 13 sustainable development teams and prioritized their social, environmental, and economic sustainability goals. During that AI Summit, the Family Members participated in a "Day of Caring," where they donated 3,720 hours of community service to make a positive impact on the local community (Fig. 6.2).

The results of their commitment at that Summit is impressive. In 2015 the Fairmount Santrol Family Members exceeded one million consecutive safe working hours for the third time in the company's history. They dedicated more than 15,000 volunteer hours to the communities in which they live and work; 30 of the facilities had achieved zero waste to landfill, an increase of 12 facilities in 2015. They invested in the planting of more than 132,000 trees in their communities (Fig. 6.3). The company also offers Family Members 40 hours of paid volunteer time a year, and empower facilities to choose their own activities or local organizations to support.

> The Sustainable Development culture reaches deep at Fairmount Santrol. Everything we do strives to nourish a stronger, more prosperous future for our company and our communities. When a company commits to contributing to the world's social, economic, and environmental needs, it can realize greater performance in all aspects of its business. From waste elimination to energy efficiency to wellness initiatives and more, sustainable development pays (Fairmount Santrol *Corporate Responsibility Report*, 2014).

Meet Chuck Fowler

Vision and values

My highest aspiration is that all the Family Members at Fairmount Santrol truly value people, the planet, and prosperity and that they are thinking beyond their individual lives. My vision is that they are living the values in their communities with their neighbors, as well as in the company. I want us to accelerate, broaden, and deepen this commitment. My hope is that our people and future Fairmount Santrol Family Members extend themselves within their communities to enable their communities to flourish.

Core values

I value the "3 Ps," people, planet, and prosperity, but I value people the most because most of our loved ones are people; without people nothing else matters. So we want people to be happy—we want them to be happy coming to work, happy at work, and happy when they go home to their families and communities. I just want them to enjoy their lives.

We held our first Appreciative Inquiry Summit in 2005 facilitated by David Cooperrider from the Weatherhead School of Management. We brought 500 people from across the company and we formalized our mission statement. We came to shared agreement that we value the 3 Ps. Now this is a fairly vague statement but it's critical for the future of the human race. As American comedian George Carlin always joked, everybody wants to save the planet, but the planet is going to be here; the question is will we be here? This is a big concern from the standpoint of our ability as human beings to exist. Without the planet none of us can prosper.

We chose prosperity because it was inclusive. We don't just want profit for the company or just fair wages for the people, we want prosperity for all of us at the company and for all of the people whose lives we touch. That is also when we came to shared agreement to be "Boldly Different" by setting bold goals for the 3 Ps, and agreed to rigorously track and measure our progress on achieving them. That is also the summit when we decided we were more than employees, we were a family, and we would call ourselves Fairmount Family Members.

Defining moments

There was an important aha! moment, the particular defining moment that set me on the path to Doing Well by Doing Good. I was about 31 years old and Vice President of Operations for Martin Marietta. We were having a difficult time with a community at one of our facilities in southwest Michigan. We were trying to get a permit for our next expansion, which was not in the dunes, but it was close enough. An activist group thought we were encroaching on the sand dunes, so they started a protest that threatened our ability to get our permits. They called us "dune rapers," which greatly affected our people that worked there. You could tell they were down in the dumps; they didn't want to be considered "dune rapers"; they wouldn't even talk to their neighbors about where they worked. There was this cloud over their heads. I went to my higher-ups in corporate in Illinois and their response was, "We'll get our lawyers right on it and we will sue them." I thought about my farming background and how my father would have dealt with this situation. I asked my higher-ups to give me a little time before they brought the lawyers in.

So we got the plant managers and the people together and asked "How can we help the community and how can the community help us?" Our people came up with the ideas and we carried them out. The most important thing we did was to just open the doors and invite the community folks in; we had an open house. The people who worked in our plant organized the event and activities to show the community what we were doing. They were the ones who lived there; their kids went to school in that community; whereas I lived in Illinois. The event was a big success. People came with their families, and the kids planted trees and dune grass. We continued to listen and get involved in the community. We are a sand company so we helped the community refurbish the beach, but again, the most important thing we did was put a sign out that said, come on in, you are welcome here!

You soon fall back on things you learned growing up in situations like this. I was the youngest of five children in a farming family from northwest Indiana., My dad was a tenant farmer and we raised livestock, corn, and other crops. My dad felt very strongly that you should take care of the land because the land takes care of you. He was a very innovative farmer yet he was very serious about the quality of the land and keeping the land in perpetuity. His name was Morton and he had a lot of Mortonisms, for example: when you are a farmer if your equipment breaks down in the middle of the afternoon you can't just run off to town to get parts, sometimes you have to Mortonize. You do what you have to do to keep moving. Farmers are great borrowers, they borrow stuff from their neighbors all the time, and they help each other a lot. Dad's adage was "Whatever you borrow take it back better than when you got it." That works not only in farming, it works in all relationships. That is why the members of the Fairmont Family take care of each other and our communities. Business is really about relationships; we make and sell products for people, so it's all about respecting for people.

Another defining moment on the road to creating Fairmount happened in 1983. I was managing the industrial sand division for Martin Marietta. We were the largest industrial sand operations in the US. I was responsible for 12 plants around the country. I was 32, the youngest plant president in Martin Marietta's history. Then Martin Marietta decided it really ought to be in the aerospace business and told the presidents of all the other businesses they owned to "go sell yourself." So my job was to sell the division, all 12 plants. The interest rate was 18% so it was tough. At the same time, while I was running around the country doing that, unfortunately our youngest daughter, Nancy, came down with melanoma cancer; she was 14. We were trying to find a treatment and at that time no one was treating adolescent cancer. We found a hospital in Houston Texas that was doing something a little in that area so Char and our daughter went there. We were living in a suburb of Chicago and we had two other daughters in high school, so it was a very difficult and emotionally challenging time for all of us. Unfortunately, we lost Nancy that spring. This was an enormous test for me about people. We had a lot of great people that helped us.

As it turned out I sold all the plants except the big one, which we could not sell because of antitrust laws. In 1985 Bill Conway of Best Sand in Cleveland and I made a deal with Martin Marietta to buy the plant. Seven of us took out second mortgages to buy the business; Bill and I went to Washington DC to get all that done. When we flew back to Chicago and drove down to the plant, a large contingent of people from the plant were waiting for us. We had a steak fry and all the people were happy even though they had just hooked their future to a startup and the prime rate was 18.5%. The people appreciated us and we appreciated them. They were excited about what was going to happen. Once again it was all about relationships. In 1986 we merged with Best Sand, located in Cleveland. That's when it became Fairmont Mineral; Bill became the CEO and I was the president and chief operating officer. That is when I decided we needed to move to Cleveland; that was our beginning. Then Bill and I decided it would be a good idea for me to go to grad school, and that's when I came to the Weatherhead School of Management. I tried to get into Harvard's Advanced Management program but they didn't accept me. That was very fortunate for me; Organizational Development was a better fit my values.

The next defining moment was 1991. I had just graduated from the Weatherhead School of Management with my MBA. We had acquired a family-owned British company. I went to David Cooperrider who was my Organizational Development professor and told him that we were trying to merge two very different company cultures. We were merging people that had not been treated very well by their company's previous owners with Fairmount, where we had worked hard to create a family culture. David had taught us that Appreciative Inquiry was an organizational development approach that was helpful in bringing people and cultures together. We brought David in and he facilitated an Appreciative Inquiry Summit and it worked very well. What I saw was that you could bring two companies that had been competitors, with very different cultures, to work together on a common mission. During the summit I saw people quickly start working together; the impact was immediate. In fact, after that first session the chief financial officer from the family-owned company we had acquired and one of our plant managers got married!

Greatest challenge along the way

That is a hard question because there hasn't been what I consider to be a hard challenge. There have been obstacles but we have overcome them. Maybe the most difficult challenge has been getting others to believe that it is possible to run a company with these values and this approach. We feel an obligation to spread this way of doing business so we invite others to our summit including our neighbors, customers, NGOs, and anyone who has an interest. We have had bird lovers participate in our summits. Kay Carter, the Executive Director of Saving Birds Thru Habitat (SBTH) in Michigan came to our 2005 Summit and the organization has have been coming ever since. She is our biggest "drumbeater," calling us the Anti-Enron. SBTH filmed a bird documentary on our properties because we have had such interesting birds on our grounds. As a result, our plants have a bird competition every year to see which facility has the most interesting birds.

Some people ask how we can afford to do this, but never our people; our Family Members understand the importance of living these values.

Most important lessons learned

One lesson I learned came from my experience with David Cooperrider and that was the power of Appreciative Inquiry and, of course, David's gifted facilitation skills.

The biggest lesson I have learned on this journey is the value of people. Given the opportunity, people are very willing to participate and they are very good at it. Their overall value, not just for what they produce for us but also the value they take to their communities, has been amazing to watch. The ballooning effect of living these values, seeing what people create out in their communities, is just incredible. The Fairmount Family Members are taking this approach to their communities and the value is multifold: the communities are not just allowing us to stay, they want us to be a part of their communities. The other critical benefit of becoming part of these communities is that we get fabulous people to join the Fairmount Santrol family. We have an 84% retention rate. So we do very well—by any measure.

What I learned from Chuck Fowler

Chuck, the leadership team and the Fairmount Santrol Family have created an environment that values people. They have extended that respect and affection to their communities and the environment. They don't simply profess to care; their actions, policies, and programs demonstrate their commitment to people and the planet. This is rare in any company but it is an extreme anomaly in the mining business. Having the courage to bring half of the employee population together every three years to co-create the future of the company speaks volumes about their trust and belief in people. Contrary to most companies in this industry who are isolated and insolated from their communities, the company invites its communities to become extended members of the Fairmount Santrol Family. It even has a bird-sighting competition with its communities in the grounds of its plants, which is a powerful testimony to the heart of the leadership and the culture of Fairmount Santrol.

Max De Pree, CEO and Chairman, 1980–95, and
D.J. De Pree, founder and CEO, 1923–62, Herman Miller

7
My journey through Camelot: a Herman Miller story

> A business is rightly judged by its products and services but it must also face scrutiny to it's humanity (D.J. De Pree, founder and CEO, 1923–62, Herman Miller).

> Our Goal is to be a Place of Realized Potential (Max De Pree, Author, *Leadership is an Art*, 1992, and former CEO and Chairman, 1980–95, Herman Miller).

The Business as an Agent of World Benefit movement is not the latest management fad nor is it a new idea. There were courageous pioneers such as Max De Pree, former CEO of Herman Miller, a Fortune 500, global office furniture company. Max and his brother and father before him, led the company with a compelling vision that was born out of a larger vision for a better world.

Herman Miller's belief in "good goods," doing well by doing good, dates back to 1927. During most of the 20th century it was not only acceptable for businesses to make money at the expense of people, families, communities and the environment, it was fashionable. Business leaders were exalted on the covers of magazines for being tough, win-at-all-cost executives. Herman Miller was an outlier; it was even considered to be heretical by many traditional capitalists. The company navigated with the core belief that people, communities and the environment *all* matter. The company struggled to make decisions and take actions that authentically valued and benefited all stakeholders. Herman Miller had the wisdom to tap into the collective gifts and creativity of the people in the company, its designers and its advisors, as well as its customers. This gave it a significant competitive edge and enabled it to prosper by innovating for the greater good.

Herman Miller was my Camelot.[1] I experienced a place where the high ideals I was taught by my parents and some of the deepest values most people cherish defined this Fortune 500 corporation. Herman Miller was a place where people dreamed big dreams together. It was a place where creativity was allowed to flourish, not just for the designers but for people in all jobs; innovation was the status quo. It was a place where people's participation was valued. We were trusted to bring our whole self to work and to contribute our unique gifts towards our shared dream of success. It was a place that honored dignity, respect, and civility, and where joy and celebration were an integral part of the culture. It was also a place of shared learning and continual transformation. I experienced Herman Miller as a place where people collectively achieved the seemingly impossible by transforming our compelling shared vision of success into reality. For me personally, Herman Miller was a place where we came close to Max De Pree's vision of "a place of realized potential … a place that liberated the human spirit."

My defining moments

During my first nine years out of college, I served in various positions in the Michigan Department of Corrections including: being one of the first two women to supervise adult men on probation in the city

---

1   Some passages in this chapter have been published in Hunt, M. (2011, April 13). Herman Miller, Inc.: My Camelot experience [Blog post]. http://michelehunt.blogspot.co.uk/2011/04/herman-miller-inc-my-camelot-experience.html and Hunt, M. (2011, April 17). The courage to live our values [Blog post]. http://michelehunt.blogspot.co.uk/2011/04/courage-to-live-our-values.html.

of Detroit; running a halfway house for female offenders; and then becoming the first female deputy warden over programs of reha-bilitation in an adult male prison in Michigan. One day I realized I was burning out, so I made the difficult decision to leave. I had wit-nessed how a negative environment could dampen the human spirit of the inmates as well as the prison staff. I felt I was "doing time." I also saw too many of my fellow civil servants unfulfilled and who at a young age were marking time for their retirement. It was time for me to get out. I decided to give the private sector a chance. Being a baby-boomer, I was very skeptical about corporations. I held the belief that all companies made money at the expense of people, fam-ilies, and communities; and they had no regard for the environment. In my search process, I was very careful and deliberate about the kind of organization to which I was willing to contribute my time, energy, and gifts; I was not willing to compromise my core values. And then I found Herman Miller.

During the interview process I was fascinated by Herman Miller because of its people. My university degrees were in sociology, so an important part of my research into companies included talking with the people that worked there. Everyone I talked to at Herman Miller lit up when they talked about the company. They rarely talked about their title or rank. They talked about "my company" like I talk about my family—with pride, honor. and love. I remember the day I decided to work for Herman Miller; it was my eighth inter-view. I was taken on a tour of its manufacturing plant in Zeeland, Michigan. To my amazement, I saw fresh flowers in the break areas. The floors were so clean they reflected the light from the windows and skylights; and yes, there were window and skylights. Everyone was on a first-name basis with my tour guide and greeted me with welcoming smiles and waves—the positive energy was palpable. As a probation officer in Detroit, I had visited many manufacturing plants and witnessed their windowless, drab conditions. I saw the despair and anger in the factory workers' eyes. There had been no joy in the places I had visited, so I was very suspicious of Herman Miller's "model factory" and I thought this must be a showroom for customers. On my way back to the interview room, I ducked into an auditorium where a meeting had just ended and observed a member of the housekeeping staff at work. She was not only putting the chairs back into place, she was meticulously working to ensure that the legs of each chair were perfectly aligned. I remember asking myself "What kind of culture and environment engenders this kind of ownership in someone who is on the bottom realm of the pay scale?" That clinched the deal! I wanted to work there. I took an entry-level job, making significantly less than my job at the prison. I also turned down three lucrative offers from other companies. I even gave up my leadership and management role to join this unusual company—basically, I started all over.

I remember the first time I met Max. It was the day before Thanksgiving and everyone met in an open area in the manufacturing plant in Zeeland, which was adjacent to Herman Miller's headquarters. I was surprised to see vice presidents casually talking with plant workers, accountants, and housekeepers. Everyone was there to celebrate Thanksgiving together. Max went to the podium and rather than read familiar platitudes, he spoke from his heart. He talked to us about people, families, and communities. He used words like love and trust. He challenged us to reach for the best in ourselves. I had always felt pressured to compartmentalize myself at work. I thought the workplace, especially the private sector, would be a difficult place to express my values. I was stunned to hear the CEO and chairman of the Board of a Fortune 500 company, telling us that it was legitimate and desirable to bring our whole self to work. When I heard Max speak of "love," "beauty," and "trust," I knew on a very deep level that I was in the right place.

In my second year at Herman Miller, I had a life-changing defining moment; a vision of life. I discovered I had five fibroid tumors in my uterus that were growing at an alarming rate. I was advised by my doctor to have a hysterectomy. On my final consultation before surgery, my doctor informed me I was pregnant and would surely die if I went through with the pregnancy. Without any discussion or even a pause, he picked up the phone and started talking with someone. He looked at me and said "I am scheduling you an abortion with a colleague of mine—I can't do it because I am Catholic." While he was talking on the phone I got up and left. On my drive home I went inside myself—much as I had many years ago when I was growing up in Kentucky and was called the "N-word." Instead of accepting the doctor's prediction for my future, I envisioned bringing my baby home and listened to my heart. I experienced calmness and I knew all would be fine. Committing to this vision changed my life forever.

During my very difficult pregnancy, I heard of a job opening that reported directly to Max De Pree, CEO and Chairman. The position, Director of Corporate Relations, was responsible for government, media, community, and shareholder relations. It was the opportunity I had been waiting for; a chance to demonstrate the leadership and management competencies I had gained in the Michigan Department of Corrections. I was eight months' pregnant at the time I applied; you could do that at Herman Miller. On the day of my interview, I went to the doctor and discovered I had developed toxemia, another serious health threat to my baby and me. My doctor immediately admitted me into the hospital. When I got to my room I called Max to inform him that I was withdrawing my bid for the job. When I explained the situation he asked, "Are you in labor?" I said "no," and then he asked "Are you in pain?" I said "no," and to my surprise, he said, "Let's interview." I got the job—and thank God, I also had my daughter, Nicole. Max comes from a community that strongly believes in traditional family values, yet he respected my decision to pursue a job while on maternity leave knowing I would have a young infant and a job that would require travel. After three months of maternity leave, I started my new job.

I soon learned a very valuable lesson: with great opportunities come great responsibilities and challenges. Just weeks after starting my new job, Max asked me to go to Washington to defeat a bill that had a good chance of passing in a subcommittee of the United States Senate. It was discreetly attached to an anti-Japanese manufacturing bill and given the climate of the country in 1981 it was likely to slide through the Senate and become law. The bill, The Retail Dealer Agreement Act, would have granted a hundred-mile exclusivity rights to Herman Miller's independent dealers. This would have limited us to one dealer per large city and crippled our distribution capacity. Shocked and in disbelief of what Max was asking me to do, I asked him if he was serious. He responded, "I hired you because I have high expectations of you and I have confidence in your abilities—go kill the bill!"

Two years later, by galvanizing the support of multiple constituents, we defeated the bill. My success was due in large part to Max's high expectations and belief in my capabilities. It was also because Max had accepted my decision and commitment to both job and baby, and I had accepted full responsibility for that decision. By doing so, we created a win–win situation. Herman Miller won and I won too. Nicole has brought me great joy and love. She is my teacher and best friend. Given who she has become today, it's apparent that Nicole won as well.

During my second year working for Max he asked me to serve as Vice President For People, responsible for global human resources, leadership development, quality and communications. I was thrilled to become an officer of the company; however, I was very uneasy with the title. I felt it was frivolous and a little corny. When I expressed my concerns, Max told me "People ought not to be regarded as human resources; money, facilities and equipment are resources—people are the heart and soul of this company." He also told me that I was not the Vice President For People, but rather "You are in the state of becoming the Vice President For People." It took years for me to understand the deep meaning and awesome responsibility inferred by that title. It was an honor to serve in that capacity.

My learning curve was steep; however, I had phenomenal teachers. Not only did Max guide me with "tough love," his father D.J. De Pree, founder of the company, helped me to understand the culture. He was 90 years old at the time and still came into the office several times a week. I was very fortunate that my office was close to his. The first thing he would say to me when he came into the office was "How is your baby?" Then he would remind me that my daughter was my priority. He would often tell me stories about how special people had influenced his values and his leadership philosophy. There were two stories D.J. shared with almost everyone who met

with him. They were what Max called "tribal stories," a way of passing on the values and culture to newcomers. The millwright story
had a profound impact on how D.J. perceived and valued employees. Here is how I recall the story:

The millwright was the craftsman who oversaw the machines
used in Herman Miller's manufacturing plant. One day the millwright died. D.J. went to visit the family. The widow invited him into
the living room and began to read aloud some beautiful poetry. D.J.
was moved by the poetry and asked who wrote it. She told him that
her husband, the millwright, was the poet.

This was a defining moment for D.J. He always wondered, was
this man who he worked with for many years, a poet who did millwright work, or a millwright who wrote poetry? This event was the
catalyst for D.J.'s quest to develop a corporate culture where people
are valued and encouraged to bring their whole self to work.

The other story he often told us was about the important role that
the designers played in helping to shape the company and his leadership approach. D.J. regarded the designers as teachers; they introduced him to design thinking. One designer who changed the course
of Herman Miller was Gilbert Rohde. In the early 1930s Herman
Miller was still making grandiose, ornate 18th-century-style furniture, and knockoffs from a different era. The country had recently
survived the Great Depression and people did not have the money,
the space or the need for the type of furniture Herman Miller was
producing. Rohde convinced D.J. that the furniture he was making
was not only irrelevant but dishonest. Rohde told D.J. "You people
think the interesting thing about furniture is furniture. The interesting thing about furniture is not furniture, it is the people who have
to live with it."

The next milestone on my journey appeared as a tremendous
obstacle. I had been in my new position a year when the company
got into trouble. We looked around and there were over 300 global
companies in our markets, making our products better, faster, and
cheaper. This was threatening over 25 years of continuous growth
and over 60 years of success. Herman Miller was regarded the best
in class. We were unmatched in design, innovation, and quality

and in sustainable financial performance. Our products were in the permanent collection of the Louvre in Paris and the Museum of Modern Art in New York; we had earned a global reputation for quality and excellence.

We learned the hard way that nothing fails like success when we fail to continuously learn and change. We had become comfortable, complacent, and even developed a touch of arrogance—a very dangerous place to be. We took our success for granted and became insulated from the changes occurring in our markets and in the world around us. We became out of touch with our customers, the changing workforce, and changes in the environment. Most damaging, we had gone off mission. We had grown so fast we were not communicating a clear direction, a vision to our employees and we were not passing on the company values. When we were small, we could pass on the vision and values through stories and relationships. Now we were large and complex and we had not adapted quickly enough—we had lost our way.

Max called for a company-wide renewal. He charged five of us on the senior leadership team to lead the renewal and made this initiative our top priority. These were people with big jobs; the Senior Vice President (SVP) of Manufacturing, the SVP of Sales and Marketing, the SVP of Research and Development, the Chief Finance Officer, and the Corporate VP For People. Max asked us to take the time to reflect on an important question: What do you believe this company ought to become? What is your vision for Herman Miller?

We secluded ourselves for a couple of days and came up with a vision, which we proudly took to Max. In his wisdom, Max knew that our vision was not sufficient. It included market share, profitability, earnings per share ... but that wouldn't get people up in the morning. It would not energize them to contribute their best to enable us to realize the vision. So Max asked us to develop a comprehensive process to engage everyone in a management role worldwide in the development of the vision.

The vision got better; however, it wasn't until we engaged every team in the company, involving every person in the company, that the vision came alive. It became richer, deeper, and better on every level. The people throughout the organization were closer to the customer and they were closer to the work; they produced, sold, and made the products. Most importantly, their involvement created a high sense of ownership for the vision. That ownership engendered commitment, energy, and excitement. The leadership team listened to all the ideas and settled on a vision "To be a Reference Point for Excellence." People wanted the company to return to a position of leadership, not purely in financial terms (although growth was essential); the emphasis was on quality, excellence, and innovation. We believed our financial performance would be a result of our collective efforts to realize our vision.

Max was still not satisfied. He believed that a vision, no matter how compelling, was not sufficient to mobilize the hearts, minds, and imagination of the people. He believed we needed a moral purpose: "Without moral purpose, competence has no measure and trust has no goal. This defining thought gives me a way to think about the place of moral purpose in our organization."

A moral purpose is defined by values. Max asked us "What values do we need to embrace in our organization to become a Reference Point for Excellence?" We repeated the participative process, engaging every person through their work-teams to help define our values. With the help of the people we came up with seven core values that would serve to shape our culture, and guide our decisions and behaviors. We also engaged everyone in companywide dialogues to insure we had shared agreement on the interpretation of those seven values. Our core values were:

- **Customer-focused vision.** Put the customer at the center of our vision.

- **Participation and teamwork.** Recognize the individual and collective genius of people. People have the right and responsibility to contribute their gifts to achieve the vision and business goals within the boundaries of our values.

- **Ownership.** Treat employees like owners emotionally and financially. Grant them stock and allow everyone to be responsible and accountable for the decisions that affect their work. Employee-owners have a right to share in the risk and rewards of the business.

- **Valuing uniqueness.** Encourage people to bring their whole self to work and to contribute their uniqueness to help achieve the company's goals. Value differences and celebrate the richness of diversity.

- **Family, social, and environmental responsibility.** Work, family, communities, and the planet are inextricable connected. Our decisions should aim for innovative solutions that support these important stakeholders.

- **Learning organization.** Invest in developing employees, leaders, and teams. Continual learning is a shared commitment.

- **Financial soundness.** Although essential, financial soundness is not the single aim of our work. It is the result of our commitment to our vision, values, and goals and our collective efforts.

The leadership team looked at the vision and values the people of Herman Miller had recommended. This led us to struggle with some very serious questions. Is it possible to achieve this vision and these values? Are they appropriate for a publically held company? In light of our economic challenges, do we have the time and resources to do this? We concluded that we must. We had to garner the courage to renew and transform the company and we needed everyone's help to get there. We developed a very disciplined companywide change process and named it "Renewal."

Participative management and ownership was a very important principle and was at the heart of the process. Herman Miller had valued and practiced employee participation since 1950; it had greatly contributed to the company's success in the past. However, as we grew larger and more complex, we had failed to continuously renew the systems, processes, and measurements necessary to sustain an effective participative management environment. Most importantly, we were drifting away from the core values that sustained the company. After just 18 months we witnessed phenomenal results: *Fortune* Magazine's Most Admired Company; *Fortune* Magazine's Top 10 Companies in America to Work for; Best Company for Women; Best Company for Working Mothers; numerous environmental awards including the White House Presidential Citation for Outstanding Environmental Management and Fortune's 10 Most Environmentally Responsible Corporations; *Business Week's* Best Products; Bertelsmann Foundation's Best Managed Company in the World. Sales increased 20% in one year and we returned to double-digit growth. We had two stock splits over the next three years

The most powerful result was in the people and culture. The energy, excitement and commitment this transformation unleashed in the people was phenomenal. People were using their minds, hearts and imagination to rethink, renew, and recreate the company. They were engaged and excited and they shared ownership for the success of the company

Now our vision and values looked like others you see on banners in corporate headquarters, in annual reports, and in marketing brochures; however, the difference was the process that got us there. We engaged everyone in the company in the development of the vision and company values and then Max had the courage to liberate the people in the organization to make the changes. We asked the employees to work in cross-functional, cross-level teams to help us change and align everything to serve our new vision, values, and business goals. We also encouraged everyone to identify anything needing to be changed through a powerful suggestion process. This process enabled the people and teams to make changes without going through a laborious hierarchy.

We moved from an organization where "quality" was a function called "quality control" to a corporate culture where "quality" became a mindset that was the standard embraced by us all. People took the vision and values very seriously. They were determined to become "A Reference Point for Excellence." Employees' pursuit of excellence was relentless. They came up with highly innovative ideas and created amazing results all across the company. In effect, we created a movement.

Participation, teamwork, and ownership

Several months into the renewal process, change was happening everywhere. People and teams felt liberated to align their work with the vision and values. This was a little frightening because they were not asking for permission and many in leadership felt we were losing control—I was one of those leaders. One day I was reading a national newspaper where we regularly placed employment ads and was surprised when I read several very unusual titles of our ads. They read:

> "My CEO believes that Trust begins at the Top—does yours?"
>
> "Does the Chairman of the Board of your company believe that leaders don't inflict pain; they bear it? Ours does."
>
> "Our goal is to be a Place of Realized Potential."

I was taken aback at first. I was the VP for People, responsible for "HR" and I had not authorized "my" recruiters to change our ads, but after reflection I realized I didn't need to be involved in that decision. A powerful concept was at play; the recruiters were serving the shared vision and values of the company; they were not there to serve me. I had learned another very important lesson; leadership is a function, not a status. My role was to create the environment that enabled employees to align the organization's policies, practices, behaviors, and results with the company's vision, values, and goals, and to remove the obstacles so they could achieve excellence.

This movement was alive with people and teams taking the ownership to make things happen all over the company including the manufacturing plants. We had won the American Airlines seating contract for its new headquarters in Dallas. A team from our seating plant delivered the chairs on a Friday, but when they unloaded them they discovered the packaging had created indentations in the backs of the chairs. American Airlines was holding its open house that upcoming Monday. The team decided to take the ownership to manually rub out the indentations in the chairs over the weekend. I am certain they violated several employment laws and they did not ask for overtime. Management did not know they had done this until several weeks later when Max received a letter from the CEO of American Airlines. You see the team had attracted the attention of people at American Airlines who were working over the weekend preparing for the open house. The Herman Miller team had also left a letter that was signed by every member of the chair assembly team. It said, "Have a wonderful open house. Thank you for being a Herman Miller Customer." That note made its way to the CEO of American Airlines, who in turn sent it to Max. We shared this story across the company. This team also inspired us to create the Outstanding Team Awards, and of course, the Dallas Chair Plant team was the first recipient.

We were about nine months into the Renewal when Max hosted a companywide meeting with 1,000 employees from around the world. The purpose was to assess our progress, to share our lessons learned, and to recharge our collective energy. Near the end of the meeting Max gave a speech praising all the hard work and accomplishments. When he finished his speech he asked if there were any questions and a young man at the back of the room raised his hand, identified himself as working in one of our manufacturing plants, and said "Max, the participative culture that you describe is not what I experience in my workplace." We were stunned that he had the gumption to raise such an objection at this open meeting. Max then explained that we were in the process of becoming a participative environment and that it takes time to change a culture. This answer did not satisfy the young man. He asked "Why do you keep promoting people who don't practice participative management into leadership positions?" He then said something that stunned us all: "What you do speaks so loudly that I cannot hear what you say." This Ralf Emerson quote powerfully resonates with me to this day. The meeting ended with us feeling very uncomfortable if not disturbed. We went back to business as usual; however, the people from that plant would not let us off the hook.

Several weeks after the companywide meeting we received a letter signed by most of the employees in that plant asking for the opportunity to work in a participative environment. This was a gift; we found the courage to acknowledge our mistake. We had not held the management of that facility accountable for living the values. I remember feeling ashamed. We were not "walking our talk" and everyone in the company knew it. The consequences of ignoring this situation could have been severe. We held a leadership meeting and decided to do the right thing. It was a liberating experience for us. Thanks to a courageous young man who took the ownership to step up and tell the truth, we learned another valuable lesson; the higher you go the less you know, so listen to those closest to the work, the customers, and the culture.

We learned to value what Max called "roving leaders"—people who assume leadership roles when the situation calls for it regardless of their level or status. Above all else, we learned that leadership's behavior and decisions must always be in alignment with the organization's vision and values to earn the trust of the people. It is impossible to create a high-performance culture that is pursuing excellence if the leaders are not aligned.

Leading with shared vision and values is a highly enlightened way to lead people. Engaging people in visioning the company's future together lifts their spirit. Engaging them in the process of transforming that compelling vision into reality touches their hearts. When people are given the opportunity to work together in teams, contributing their ideas and gifts, and being valued and recognized for their contribution, they accomplish amazing things, and love doing so. This creates a win–win–win experience and gives meaning to work.

Family, social, and environmental responsibility

Family, social, and environmental responsibility was the most revolutionary of all the values at the time, especially for a publicly traded Fortune 500 company. I was sure that these values would cause the toughest debates and hardest decisions among the leadership team; I was wrong. The team was very engaged and proud of these values. They helped us to see the inextricable connection between the company and people, families, communities, and the environment. We made courageous and radical decisions to align our policies and practices and behaviors with these important values.

On one occasion, we were discussing our high-performing, high-potential leaders and decided it was time to promote one of the best and the brightest in the company. Vicki TenHagen had a proven track record of success and everyone had the highest respect for her leadership qualities; she exemplified the company values. This was an easy decision. When we approached her with a vice presidential position, she declined. Vicki had recently had her second child and decided that with two children under three years old, she needed to work part time. We understood but we were disappointed. I remember the leadership dialogue that followed. Phil Mercarella, our SVP of Sales and Marketing came up with a win–win–win solution. Herman Miller made innovative furniture designed for offices and yet many customers were purchasing our products for their homes. We had been talking for months about creating a division that sold our products for use in homes. Phil suggested we promote Vicki to general manager to lead Herman Miller for the Home and honor her desire to work part time.

Vicki and her team held most of their meetings at her home, allowing her to nurture her children. It also allowed the team to develop the strategies for products and services within an authentic home environment. This gave them a tremendous advantage. They successfully developed the products, services, and business plan, surpassing our expectations in cost, time, and quality. When I asked Vicki years later what it was like to be a "part-time" general manager charged with launching a brand new product line, she said it was a wonderful experience. Her life was very integrated. She did not have to compartmentalize or juggle between family and work. She said,"My children use to think that all families visited furniture stores when they went on vacation—it was just my life."

I experienced Herman Miller's commitment to family in a very personal way. A very disturbing event happened in my daughter's life that led me to the conclusion that I had to leave Herman Miller and move my daughter to Chicago. After my daughter was born I thought I could be a superwoman, I thought I could handle it all. But things got complicated after my divorce. I went through four nannies in six weeks. The first nanny was taking my daughter on her house-to-house sales calls, selling Avon cosmetics. The second and third nannies were more interested in entertaining their boyfriends than attending to my daughter. Even during these tough times, I was able to "keep it together." At Herman Miller it was not uncommon for Nicole to spend the day playing in my office. My assistant, Donna Kowe, loved her like a family member and my colleagues in corporate office were like her extended family. Even as a single parent, it seemed I was able to be a nurturing mother and have a successful career.

One day that all changed; I woke up to a new reality. I saw all my decisions about my child, my job, and my home as bad decisions. I was a failure. My primary responsibility in life was to protect and nurture my daughter and to create a safe, positive environment for her to learn, grow, and develop. This day, this defining event, made it apparent I was failing at the most important job of my life. Nicole was in the first grade. I was walking her to the school bus and she abruptly stopped. Surprised, I turned around and saw a look of sadness in her eyes, a look I had never seen on her face. She said to me "Mom, I don't want to take the bus." I asked why and she said "The kids are mean to me." Nicole was a very sociable child and loved riding the school bus with the other children. She also had a strong personality, even at the age of six, so I was very surprised. She went on to tell me that all the children told her she belonged at the back of the bus. I was confused because these were great kids that Nicole had known all her life. Next, she said something that nearly floored me. She told me there were two paintings in the hall across from the principal's office; one painting showed a bus full of children with black kids sitting in the back and the caption said "Negros belong at the back of the bus"; the other picture was a yellow cafe with a sign on the door, "No Negros allowed." In a state of disbelief, I took Nicole to school, walked to the hall outside of principal's office, and there they were, the two pictures just as Nicole had described. In that moment, my world turned upside down. Memories of my childhood living in Kentucky rose up in me. We were the only Black family living in a small town in Western Michigan, but I thought the days when this behavior was acceptable were long past. There was no way I was going to allow my daughter to suffer that pain and humiliation.

I went to work that day and quit my job. I told my teammates and the president of the company what had happened and that I had to take my daughter to a more diverse, inclusive environment. Several weeks later we were off to Chicago. The beautiful thing was that Herman Miller found a win–win solution for me to keep my job and live in Chicago. I kept my responsibilities and took on a special assignment to help the company develop minority suppliers. This allowed me to work from Chicago and commute to the corporate headquarters for meetings. My team stepped up and filled in the gaps; some were promoted because they took on more leadership responsibilities. This ended up being a win for us all.

Environmental responsibility

The decisions we made about being environmentally responsible were radical at that time. Herman Miller was one of the first companies in the world to implement a smoke-free policy. In 1986 the senior leadership made this decision but we went to the people to implement it. We established a cross-level, cross-function, cross-geography action team. This team was charged with developing the process and the practices necessary to implement this difficult goal. Within several weeks they came to us with an integrated, thoughtful, doable plan. It included a smoke cessation and education programs for those who wanted to quit smoking and a six-month phased implementation timetable. As impressive as this plan was, we in leadership still thought it would be very difficult to implement—it wasn't! People all over the company took ownership for the outcome.

Several months after we created a smoke-free environment, I received a call from the president of one of the major cigarette companies. He had read in one of our national employment ads that we provided a smoke-free environment. He was angry! He told me that he had a $10 million contract for Herman Miller furniture on his desk and that he would not sign it until we rescinded our no smoking policy. The leadership team held an emergency meeting to discuss the situation. I anticipated a lot of debate; in fact, I believed my colleagues would choose money over values. I was wrong! The meeting lasted about 20 minutes. The team unanimously decided to stay the course and potentially forfeit the contract. It was not only the right thing to do; it made good business sense. If we had rescinded the policy, we would have lost the trust of the people and proved that leadership was not aligned with the values. The cumulative cost of losing people's trust would have been incalculable and possibly not recoverable. Max always reminded us "Trust is built on kept promises."

Our values applied to our products and services as well as our people. The Eames Lounge Chair was designed by Charles and Ray Eames and manufactured by Herman Miller in 1956. Setting the standard for elegance and comfort, it is considered among the most significant furniture designs of the 20th century and is in the permanent collection of New York's Museum of Modern Art. The Eames Lounge Chair was originally produced with a rosewood veneer. In 1991 Herman Miller stopped using rosewood believing that we were contributing to the decline of the Brazilian rainforest. This was a very difficult and controversial decision to make from a design integrity standpoint, as well as a sales and marketing perspective. However, it was the right thing to do. Herman Miller was far ahead of its time. The concept of a "green company" would not come into being until almost ten years after Herman Miller made this environmentally conscious decision. The Government of Brazil now controls rosewood as an endangered species. Once again, we had the courage to be true to our values, and we were right.

Herman Miller's commitment to building "green buildings" dates back to D.J. De Pree's leadership. He instituted the facilities design criteria that any new properties that the company developed had to have 50% or more "green space." The criterion also stipulated that the buildings must compliment the surrounding environment

FIGURE 7.1 Herman Miller's facilities are built in confluence with the architecture in their surrounding communities and with nature

(Fig. 7.1). He also mandated that all employees should be able to look out of a window no further than 75 feet away. This included manufacturing facilities. Today it is known that harvesting natural daylight cuts energy bills, reduces pollution and energizes people.

Having the courage to include family, social and environmental responsibility in our values brought out the best in us. This set of values helped us to learn that we had the capacity to do good and do well. It helped us to see and understand the inextricable connections between people, families, communities and the environment. It helped us understand our responsibilities beyond profits. We became acutely aware that we were a part of a greater chain of events and a greater whole. Personally, it was an exciting, beautiful, and deeply fulfilling way to work.

Leadership: a radical departure

> Leadership is a serious meddling in other people's lives
> (Max De Pree).

The critical ingredient to Herman Miller's success was a leadership philosophy that was rooted in the basic belief that people are extraordinary and capable of achieving remarkable things. We abandoned the traditional assumptions that people are lazy, can't be trusted, and have limits to their growth. We valued our people, customers, and shareholders *and* we believed that families, communities, and the planet were important stakeholders in our business. This had enormous implications for those of us who had leadership responsibilities. Our leadership and management decisions and behaviors needed to reflect our values and beliefs.

Equity was one of those beliefs. "Inclusive capitalism" was a serious commitment that embodied the concept that meritocracy applied to everyone. We instituted some bold policies and programs to align our actions:

- **CEO pay.** Max De Pree had the courage and the character to limit the size of the CEO's base salary to 20 times the base of the average employee's salary. He believed there should be an equitable connection, a relationship a between the CEO's pay and the employees' pay as well as a direct relationship between the company's performance and the leaders' pay.

- **The silver parachute.** Max established this revolutionary policy. Rather than having a "golden parachute," which entitled the CEO and top executives to receive a lot of money if we lost our jobs from an unfriendly takeover, the silver parachute entitled *all* employees who lost their jobs from a hostile takeover to receive a healthy financial package. This was a win–win–win solution as the acquiring company had to factor in this potential cost.

- **Monthly business reviews.** We empowered everyone with information that is reserved for leadership in most organizations. The Senior Leadership Team held monthly business reviews to share information (the good, the bad, and the ugly) with all employees. We videotaped the reviews and all work-team leaders were accountable to share the videos with their teams and discuss ways they could contribute. Transparency was essential and non-negotiable. Communications were abundant, predictable, and accessible to all employees and teams. Everyone knew the corporate goals and priorities and the status of our progress. This enabled the work teams to celebrate the good news and to put a laser focus on the problem areas. This also required that everyone become "business literate," so we provided education on the fundamentals of business to all employees.

- **Our earned share.** Unlike most companies who only give bonuses to executives, everyone from the janitor to the CEO shared in a companywide quarterly bonus called "Our earned share" when we collectively outperformed our shared corporate goals. Those bonuses sometimes exceeded 30% of employees' quarterly gross salaries. People rarely let us down; more often than not, they exceeded our expectations. They did not act as subordinates or employees—they acted like owners

Our commitment to family, social and environmental responsibility resulted in great benefits to everyone who was a part of the Herman Miller family. We attracted the best and the brightest people—not because we paid the most, because of our commitment to the quality of life for all our stakeholders. People were proud to work at Herman Miller and became our greatest recruiters and public relations. Local governments and communities were constantly in pursuit of having Herman Miller expand into their communities. In the long run, we learned that being socially responsible was not only the right thing to do, it also made good business sense.

Leadership was an awesome responsibility. We understood our purpose and our power. We understood the great good and the great harm we could do to people, families, communities, and the environment. We were not just accountable to shareholders—we were accountable to a myriad of interwoven stakeholders.

To become a leader at Herman Miller, we had to unlearn almost everything we had been taught in business school. This was not easy. To move from seeing leadership as a status to embracing it as a service, took a dramatic shift in mindset. To help us make that transition and to remind us of our leadership responsibility, Max commissioned a sculpture of a Water Carrier created by Allan Houser, a Native American painter and modernist sculptor. He had it placed in the corporate center courtyard. Max had a small version of the sculpture placed outside the office of the CEO, as a symbol of our values and beliefs. The inscription read: "The tribal water carrier in this corporation is a symbol of the essential nature of all jobs, our interdependence, the identity of ownership and participation, the servanthood of leadership, and the authenticity of each individual."

The magic of Herman Miller was its people and our leadership philosophy, which was born out of our vision and core values. The values were the key ingredient, the yeast that helped everyone rise to the challenge. They embodied all that is truly important in life. Our commitment was to treat people with dignity and respect and to create an environment worthy of people's commitment. We struggled daily to align our words, actions, and decisions with our values and beliefs. We made mistakes, we lost our way from time to time, but our values served as a powerful force that pulled us back on course. Collectively the people of Herman Miller created an extraordinary company that became "A reference point for excellence, by almost any measure." I finally understood the awesome responsibility of becoming Vice President For People.

What I learned from Herman Miller, Inc.

I was blessed to have worked at Herman Miller. I experienced a very evolved form of leadership and saw the tremendous benefits of true democratic capitalism at work. We were far ahead of our time. What Max calls "a place of realized potential" is a place I call Camelot! Although many of us are no longer at Herman Miller we carry the spirit of Herman Miller in our hearts and try to live what we learned in our lives, our work, and our communities; so the legacy lives on. Herman Miller helped to prepare me for the transformative times we are living in today. I gained the experience and skills to contribute to the Business as an Agent for World Benefit movement, for which I am deeply grateful. I experienced firsthand, a company that prospered by innovating for the greater good.

Part 2
Blurring the lines

Gunhild Stordalen giving the opening address at the 2015 EAT Forum

8
The EAT Initiative: world-changing food for thought

> Providing the growing global population with a healthy and nutritious diet within safe environmental limits is one of the greatest challenges facing humanity today. It can only be addressed through an integration of knowledge and action in the interwoven areas of food, health and sustainability (Dr. Gunhild A. Stordalen MD/PhD, founder and President of EAT Foundation, cofounder and Chair, Stordalen Foundation).

Randi Skaamedal, a dear friend and colleague of mine from Oslo, Norway, knows that I have an insatiable passion for shining a light on DreamMakers, so when she learned about Gunhild Stordalen's fascinating story, she strongly encouraged me to write about her. I had finished interviewing people and, quite honestly, I had no interest in adding more stories to the book. Even in the face of multiple nagging text messages from Randi to take a look at Gunhild's work, my mind was made up, case closed. Then synchronicity came into play, I was searching for a video on YouTube and a video of Gunhild giving opening remarks at the 2015 EAT Stockholm Food Forum popped up in the right column of my screen. I listened to her compelling presentation, which awakened me to the broken global food system crisis, and by the time she had finished I was part of the movement. Gunhild is an amazing visionary leader with an unshakeable commitment to advance the "transformation of the global food system to sustainably feed a healthy population of nine billion people by mid-century."

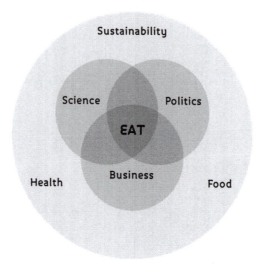

FIGURE 8.1   The nexus of food, health, and sustainability
Source: EAT website.

Dr. Gunhild Stordalen's vision is bold, aggressive, and courageous, and her unwavering optimism, unmovable will, and strong sense of urgency are the essential characteristics to usher this world-changing vision into reality. Gunhild wants to do no less than save the world, and she believes that collectively we can do just that! I feel honored to help share this inspiring DreamMaker's story.

Gunhild has unapologetically dedicated her life to transforming one of the most complex, socially, economically, and politically charged global challenges facing people and the planet in the 21st century—the global food system. She has a deep understanding of and appreciation for the inextricable connections between food production, consumption, and distribution and the impact they have on the health and well-being of people and the planet. She believes that transforming the global food system is the highest leverage opportunity and most cost-effective way to ensure a healthy, sustainable future.

To seize this opportunity, Gunhild founded the EAT Initiative in 2013 under the Stordalen Foundation, in partnership with the Stockholm Resilience Centre at the University of Stockholm. The

EAT Initiative is a global platform and an international consortium of world leading academic and research institutions, governments, businesses, philanthropic foundations, and nonprofit organizations. Together they hold a shared understanding that it is essential to address the challenges of food, health, and sustainability, through a collective, collaborative, and holistic approach, to enable more than 9 billion people and the planet to flourish by 2050. EAT's mission, vision, strategies, and research are closely linked to the UN Sustainable Development Goals.

The Stordalen Foundation was founded by Gunhild and her husband, Petter Stordalen, to "support projects, initiatives and organizations that work for a healthy and sustainable future." The Stockholm Resilience Centre serves as EAT's primary academic partner. It is a leading research center on global sustainability that focuses on resilience: "the ability of a system to deal with change and continue to develop." Other EAT partners include CGIAR Consortium, Harvard School of Public Health, New York Academy of Sciences, the Sackler Institute of Nutrition Science, Berkley Food Institute University of California, Harvard Global Equity Initiative, Cornell University Food and Brand Lab Science, University College London Institute for Global Health, and the Norwegian Institute of Public Health.

> Scientific research being at the heart of the EAT Initiative, the centrepiece of its structural architecture is a network of world leading universities and research institutions, with the common objective of advancing knowledge and identifying synergistic solutions within the nexus of food, health and sustainability (EAT website).

In addition to cross-disciplinary research, each year EAT hosts EAT Stockholm Food Forum, a high-level, cross-sector forum that brings together international stakeholders, including leading scientists from different disciplines, policymakers, business executives and leaders from civil society, to engage in dialogue and debate, catalyze innovations, facilitate new partnerships, and collaboratively develop holistic solutions to the global food system challenge: "Population growth, climate change, human health, resource management, sustainability and food security are independent fields of science and research but they are also important political issues which represent new business opportunities" (EAT Stockholm Food Forum, 2015).

Gunhild's personal story is as inspirational and valiant as her vision. In 2014, a year after launching the EAT Initiative, she contracted systemic scleroderma, a rare, life-threatening autoimmune disease. While struggling with this disease and the challenges of the severe treatment, she continued to actively advance her vision and work to further EAT's mission. Those who work with her were astounded by her commitment and tenacity:

> When Gunhild was laying there flat, vomiting, basically unable to communicate and delegate things to the EAT Team, we were trying to hold her at a distance but in fact, my mobile was blipping two or three times everyday with EAT related text messages. I would argue that EAT was part of Gunhild's medication because even as she was undergoing the most severe chemotherapy, her engagement was extraordinary (Professor Johan Rockström, Executive Director of the Stockholm Resilience Centre).

After undergoing intense stem cell transplantation (HSCT) plus high-dose chemotherapy the autoimmune disease went into remission and Gunhild was on the road to resuming her life. But one year later, she experienced a serious relapse. Yet she has faced the return of her disease with the same unshakable optimism, courage, and tenacity that she does in advancing her bold vision to transform the global food system. In fact, Gunhild believes the EAT initiative is, in part, responsible for her strong will to overcome the disease. She has a world-changing life purpose and over the last year she has made tremendous progress advancing that mission even in the face of her illness.

Gunhild has also been very open and candid about her condition. She was awarded the Norwegian Women Public Health Association (NKS) Fredrikke Price Award in 2014, 2015, and 2016, Environmental Hero of the Year by WWF Sweden, and in 2014 she was ranked among the 100 most influential Norwegian Women by the financial magazine *Kapital* for her efforts in food security and sustainable development and for being transparent about her disease. She used the prize money from the award to bring a group of Ethiopian women, who work with food security and sustainability in their local communities, to the 2016 EAT Stockholm Food Forum. Gunhild believes the key to change is to strengthen the position of women in developing countries: "When women receive money, 90% of it goes to ensure nutrition, health and education and therefore lifts families out of poverty."

When I interviewed Gunhild for this book, I personally witnessed her commitment to EAT. At the beginning of the interview she revealed to me that she had recently experienced a relapse, "the scleroderma has come back but I'm not giving up," yet in the face of this challenge she opted to share her story. Her passion and engagement during this interview were extraordinary.

Meet Gunhild Stordalen

Vision and values

Healthy people and a healthy planet. EAT's vision is a world where everybody has the knowledge needed to make smart and sustainable food decisions, the access needed to eat a responsible and healthy diet and the inspiration needed to adopt this behavior across their lifestyle.

We are in the middle of a crisis that's "eating us up.". Millions of people around the world don't have enough to eat—meanwhile millions more are eating too much at great risk to themselves and the environment. In an effort to produce enough food for our growing population we are causing irreversible damage to the planet. This situation is unsustainable and if you think it's bad now, imagine what it will be like in a world of 9 billion people. Political, scientific, and business experts have searched for solutions in isolation for too long and it's holding us all back. If we're going to solve our global food crisis before it's too late, we need to work together to change the entire food system—and we need to do it now.

Unfortunately, the current global food system is broken. Food production is the single most important driver of greenhouse gas emissions and environmental degradation, more people die from too much food than from too little, and unhealthy diets have leapfrogged smoking as the most important factor for disease globally. Although we are producing enough calories to feed more than the world's current population it is not equally distributed; we throw away one-third of what is being produced. According to the World Hunger Organization, 800 million people in the world go hungry every night. Furthermore, it is not always economically possible or convenient for people to make the right food choices. In certain regions and many communities around the world fresh healthy food is not available. People often have to travel to the other end of town to buy the right tomatoes—for a higher price. Knowing that our food purchasing behavior to a great extent is driven by price, taste and availability, you can never expect these conditions to foster sustainable healthy food choices. We need to make fundamental societal changes to transform how and what the world grows and produces and what the world's population eats.

The ultimate vision of EAT is to be able to feed more than 9 billion healthy people by the year 2050 in a healthy sustainable manner. In other words, to eradicate world hunger and malnutrition, tackle the epidemics of obesity and chronic diseases such as heart disease, diabetes type II, and cancer *and* to avoid irreversible climate change, degradation of ecosystems, and the impact on the planet's biodiversity. This of course is a huge and multifaceted challenge but at the same time, I believe it is the biggest opportunity for humanity to concurrently invest in better human and planetary health through better prevention and mitigation rather than the hitherto "reactive" focus on adaptation, treatment, and repair in today's society. As a medical doctor, I find it shocking to look back and think of the almost nonexistent role of preventive medicine in the curriculum. Instead, medical school was all about treatment and repair, how to develop new drugs for illnesses or how to develop new surgical techniques. No pill or new surgical technique will ever take us out of the public health crisis we are in today and will face in the future if we do not change.

Up until now we have focused our efforts and initiatives in silos. The health community has been looking into nutrition and public health. The climate scientist and the agricultural scientist have been looking into the environmental impact of food and food production. We have failed to look at the bigger picture and acknowledge all the inevitable interlinkages between food, health, and the environment, and of course the linkages to social justice and economic development. All these issues are connected.

To address this huge challenge, EAT has launched four core objectives to help transform the food system while positively impacting climate change and sustainability:

First, we work to **map out the existing knowledge gaps in the food–health–sustainability nexus and initiate new interdisciplinary research projects** across EAT's academic network. This will help increase the understanding of the many interlinks, the synergies, and the trade-offs between human health and the environment when it comes to diets and food production. We have a lot of existing data but substantial knowledge gaps exist across the many interlinks. Therefore, driving more interdisciplinary research is a fundamental role of EAT.

Second, we are working to **translate existing evidence into action**, that is, to develop a better decision-making platform for policymakers for the implementation of efficient policy instruments—regulations, incentives, and taxes—to support this transformation. In particular, we are working to encourage the food industry—farmers, retailers, food producers, food service industry and all the different stakeholders in the food value chain—to promote healthy, sustainable food production and distribution.

Third, we **recognize that while business is part of the problem, it is also a key part of the solution**. Business leaders act on facts, and hence, we want to work closely with the business community, the food industry, and all their stakeholders to help them access new data and be able to translate global risks into business opportunities. Profit making is necessary for the world to move forward. If businesses go bankrupt, they cannot contribute their innovations and resources to help transform the system. So it is critically important to show that it is possible to make money from producing, distributing, and serving sustainable healthy food.

This win–win scenario is vital to the transformation of the global food system. In addition, emerging markets and new demands will require us to develop healthier, reformulated products that don't come with a huge environmental cost and don't make people sick.

Fourth, we are **developing strategies for changing consumer behavior *at scale*.** In addition to providing consumers with better and simpler information about healthy and sustainable food choices, we need to take a systemic approach to influencing society. We have created an obesogenic environment where we are continuously surrounded by cheap, unhealthy, and easily available foods loaded with lots of added sugars and fats and often served in huge portions. You can never expect these conditions to foster sustainable, healthy food choices. This is a very complex and ambitious agenda; however, we believe it is possible. We need to learn from the fight against Big Tobacco. It took more than four decades, plus a plethora of tactics including advertising, marketing, education, and finally a ban, to reduce the number of daily smokers in the US by 50%. While every cigarette is bad for you, food consumption is much more complex and challenging and requires multi-stakeholder communication, collaboration, and coordination.

The United States is the second largest contributor to climate change and environmental degradation in the world. US meat consumption is about to become an even greater threat to the environment than our cars. New research supports the fact that the world's livestock industry is not just a large contributor to climate change, accounting for almost 15% of the world's annual emissions, it is also extremely resource inefficient, in addition to driving deforestation, loss of biodiversity, and depletion of scarce fresh water reserves. Meat consumption per capita increases with increasing affluence—hence the increasing appetite for meat and dairy in emerging economies such as China and India is of even bigger concern; at the rate we are going meat production will have to double by 2050 to meet the expected demand. In the United States and most other developed countries around the world, people consume large amounts of cheap meat despite the unrefuted evidence of the devastating environmental and health consequences of producing and consuming high volumes of red meat. This is not sustainable for either people or the planet.

In spite of the strong recommendations from the US Dietary Guidelines Advisory Committee to include "sustainability goals" in the *Dietary Guidelines for Americans 2015–2020*, they were left out. In a joint statement US Department of Agriculture Secretary Tom Vilsack and Sylvia Burwell, Secretary of Health and Human Services, said "We do not believe that the 2015 DGAs [Dietary Guidelines for Americans] are the appropriate vehicle for this important policy conversation about sustainability." The US signed the UN Sustainability Development Goals in the Paris agreement in 2015, which includes ending all forms of malnutrition around the world and ensuring sustainable food security, yet it failed to include the environmental impact of food on human health and the planet in the dietary guidelines for Americans. On one hand the United States publicly advocates to irradiate global malnutrition and yet ignores one of the greatest health and environmental threats to people and the planet.

This is an extremely unfortunate situation and the sad thing is that most of this can be prevented. There has been too little focus on the relationship between food systems, public health, and the environment. We must fix the broken global food system if we are to succeed in creating a sustainable future. The long-term cost of not taking action is not sustainable; the epidemic of diet-related chronic diseases is expected to cost the world economy upwards of US$47 trillion over the next two decades unless urgent action is taken. We need to help society shift this behavior and this will take multi-stakeholder, cross-disciplinary and multinational cooperation and collaboration. Our whole society needs to rethink how we solve global threats. We need to move from a reactive mentality to a mindset of prevention. Whenever possible, this is always the better and most cost-effective option both for the individual and for society. Creating a healthy, more sustainable global food system is one of our biggest opportunities for leveraging multiple win–wins and the closest we get to a silver bullet that will simultaneously improve the health of people and planet.

Defining moments

I was raised by academic parents on a small farm in the countryside of Norway. As a child, my parents taught me to love the beauty of nature and the value of biodiversity. They taught my siblings and me about animals, birds, fish, flowers, and plants, and how these extremely beautiful, finely tuned bio-systems were the fundamentals for human health and well-being and for a sustainable future. They also introduced us to the huge footprint we are leaving behind and how we are destroying the essence for humanity by polluting. My mom supplemented her grocery shopping with home-produced food; we grew tomatoes, raised free range chickens, and had lots of pets. I learned to respect all kinds of life as family members, not just humans. I felt incredibly sad that innocent animals were treated so badly in the industrialized livestock industry. I decided I wanted to ensure that people woke up to ethically and socially respecting animals and all life so I considered becoming a veterinarian. But I quickly learned that if you are a vet you become a part of the factory-farm meat production system and that your role is not to protect animals but rather to increase the farmers' profit potential, with little or no regard for the animals' health and welfare. I decided to find another way to become an advocate for animal welfare and help to bring more social justice to the world; I became a medical doctor like my mom.

I decided in my early childhood that I want to use my voice to make a difference in the world. My parents taught me that no one can do everything but everyone can do something. So when I was six or seven, I started selling my toys to raise money for the Rainforest Foundation in Norway and I organized protest marches against pollution with the kids in the neighborhood. I felt I was making an impact.

Then, in 1987 the Montreal Protocol on Substances that Deplete the Ozone Layer was approved by all of the members of the United Nations. Its goal was to reduce and ultimately phase out the production and consumption of substances that are depleting the earth's ozone layer. The Montreal Protocol is one of the greatest global environmental achievements in human history. The global community came together and effectively solved the ozone threat. Today, 26 years after the signing of the Montreal Protocol, the global community has phased out 98% of ozone-depleting substances and every country in the world is in compliance with the agreement. I realized at a young age that we can collectively change the world and I decided to dedicate my life to making a difference. I felt that my purpose, my mission in life, was to do as much as I could for the time I am alive, to make the world a better place.

Then, in 2006, Al Gore's book, *An Inconvenient Truth*, was a wake-up call for me and most people around the world.[1] Climate change became a new global challenge. I decided I would help mitigate climate change so I started working for various climate change organizations.

The next defining moment was when I met my beloved husband, Petter. My parents didn't care about material things, they were focused on social justice and moral values. They always had old, ugly cars, they were anti-materialistic and focused on being good human beings. These were the core values that they passed on to their kids. After I married, I told my husband I was not a diamond girl so I didn't want diamonds for my wedding gift. Instead, I asked him for approval to establish a foundation in our name. If we died in a plane crash, I wanted to ensure that our vision and beliefs about helping to create a sustainable future for people and the planet would be continued. He thought it was a beautiful idea and we started the Stordalen Foundation from which I birthed the EAT Initiative in 2013.

Today, action is being taken and a lot is happening to mitigate climate change. Fortunately, the climate deniers are now in danger of becoming extinct. A huge defining moment for the world happened at the historic UN Sustainable Development Summit in Paris in September 2015, when the world leaders agreed to 17 Sustainable Development Goals to end poverty, fight inequality and injustice, and tackle climate change by 2030. Unfortunately, the commitments made by the world's leaders in Paris are not sufficient to reach the new target of limiting global warming down towards 1.5 degrees and only take us half way there. But the world food system is the missing link. It is so shocking that food is not even included

1   Gore, A. (2006). *An Inconvenient Truth: The Planetary Emergency of Global Warming and What We Can Do About It*. Emmaus, PA: Rodale Press.

in the equation. We know that global food production is causing up to
30% of human-made climate emissions and still we don't have a roadmap
for what food systems—from country to country—will have to look like in
2050. We have a 2050 roadmap for energy systems, we have a roadmap
for transportations systems but not for food systems. This is a huge
concern. We have three critical mitigation opportunities that in particular will
benefit public health: cleaner energy, smarter walkable cities with public
transportation systems, and a healthy sustainable global food system.

Unhealthy diets have surpassed smoking as the biggest killer and
the greatest risk factor for human disease on a global basis, and our
diets have a tremendous impact on the climate and the environment.
So establishing global norms of healthy diets from sustainable food
production systems is the only way forward to ensure long-term food
security and a sustainable, prosperous future for all.

Milestones and progress

EAT started out as a local breakfast seminar in Oslo in 2013 and in
less than 12 months it exploded into a multi-stakeholder, cross-discipline
global initiative. Five hundred leaders and experts from 28 countries
gathered at the inaugural EAT Forum in 2014, including heads of state,
UN representatives, prominent thought leaders from the fields of science,
politics, business, and civil society, and President Bill Clinton among the
speakers. The year after, the second EAT Forum in June 2015 gathered
the same number of delegates from 31 countries. In the meantime,
the EAT network expanded substantially and now consists of around 70
partners from around the globe, from Harvard, Berkeley, and Cornell
universities, and NY Academy of Sciences, to University College London
and University of Oslo and Stockholm, to multinational conglomerates
such as Google, Deloitte, Tetra Pak, and Nestlé.

To advance the mission of EAT, the UK charitable foundation, the
Wellcome Trust, was invited to join forces and together with the Stordalen
Foundation and the Stockholm Resilience Centre, co-founded the
EAT Foundation in March 2016. The Wellcome Trust, whose aim is to
"achieve extraordinary improvements in health by supporting the brightest
minds," is the second largest charitable foundation in the world. The

core objective of the EAT Foundation is to drive new interdisciplinary knowledge and facilitate the translation of that knowledge into policy development and business actions. To catalyze a transformative shift in the global food system that delivers healthy nutrition to a rapidly growing world population, we need urgent multi-stakeholder efforts across sectors and disciplines that can deliver high impact, realistic solutions that can be put into practice within a short time frame. The foundation's scientific work is focused on three areas: metrics for health and sustainable food, multifunctional landscapes and seascapes, and consumer behavior and choices. The development of the EAT Foundation is a major milestone on EAT's journey. It gives it the ability to exponentially advance the EAT vision. "A healthy planet is the only option if we want to provide healthy diets for nine billion people, conversely healthy diets will support a healthy planet. This is the virtuous circle at the heart of the EAT Foundation" (Johan Rockström, Chairman, EAT Advisory Board, Executive Director, Stockholm Resilience Centre).

The annual EAT Stockholm Food Forum, is another major achievement of the EAT initiative. We bring together some of the world's brightest people in the fields of science, politics, business, and civil society to shift food systems towards greater sustainability, health, security, and equity within the boundaries of our planet.

Research is the centerpiece of the EAT initiative. We have launched several research projects with Harvard, Oxford, and Cornell Universities and in May 2015 we published *Reviewing Interventions for Healthy and Sustainable Diets*[2] in partnership with the Centre on Global Health Security at Chatham House, the Royal Institute of International Affairs independent policy institute based in London. It provides an overview of the state of the global food system and the affect it is having on the health and well-being of people and the planet, as well as strategies and interventions that are being developed to transform the food system.

We are in the process of developing a Global Food Database, which will be an interactive repository of data on indicators that collectively track progress toward diets that are both healthy and sustainable. It will

2   Bailey, R. and Harper, D. (2015). *Reviewing Interventions for Healthy and Sustainable Diets*. London: Chatham House.

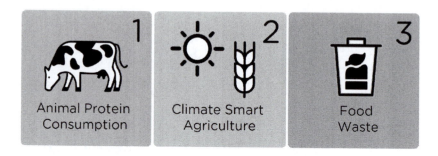

FIGURE 8.2   Priority indicators for achieving sustainable development

Source: EAT Forum, http://eatforum.org/article/integrated-indicators-for-sustainable-food-systems-and-healthy-diets, September 24, 2015.

be an open-access and freely downloadable database that serves as a comprehensive and intelligible self-learning platform for food industry leaders, policymakers, scientists, civil society organizations, and the general public.

The EAT Initiative, the Sustainable Development Solutions Network and CGIAR Consortium have proposed a set of 11 integrated indicators for monitoring progress towards achieving healthy diets from sustainable food systems under the existing Sustainable Development Goals framework, which includes the three priority indicators that are considered to be the most crucial to achieving overall sustainable development[3] (see Fig. 8.2):

- Priority indicator 1: Animal Protein Consumption—per capita animal protein consumption and per capita land requirement for animal protein consumption.

- Priority indicator 2: Climate Smart Agriculture—carbon emissions from agricultural land use (tons per hectare per year).

- Priority indicator 3: Food Waste—% of food loss and waste from food production to consumption and % of food waste recycled.

3   EAT, Sustainable Development Solutions Network, and CGIAR (2015). *Integrated Indicators for Sustainable Food Systems and Healthy Diets in the Post-2015 Development Agenda Final Statement September 17th 2015*, p. 10. Retrieved from https://library.cgiar.org/bitstream/handle/10947/4011/17th%20Sept%20Final%20Statement%20on%20SDG%20indicators%20EAT-SDSN-CGIAR.pdf?sequence=1.

Obstacles

The broken global food system is the result of a systemic failure; no single sector or player can be hold solely responsible. Part of the problem is caused by failed agricultural subsidies (particularly in the US) after the Second World War, where the problem was a lack of food. The unbalanced subsidies to giant monocrops of a few staples—including wheat, soy, and corn, the main ingredients in fast food and for animal feed—along with new processing techniques have resulted in an overproduction of highly profitable cheap calories at the expenses of producing fresh natural foods. The US food industry contributed $800 billion to the US economy in 2013. It is in the economic interest of the food producers as well as the US economy to protect the status quo. They also have an enormous impact on the European economy. Capitalist forces must be understood and taken into consideration; companies are inevitably dependent on making profit to survive. Hence, governments must lead the transition, put the right regulations and incentives in place, and set the agenda. But in order to catalyze such a shift, we need all stakeholders to arrive at a common understanding on the urgency of the situation and what is needed to be done. Therefore, we have to create a platform to bring the multinational food giants to the table to engage in genuine dialogue on how we can collaboratively transform the global food system and still enable companies to profit. Most companies know they have to change and that it is in everyone's interest to engage in co-creating a healthy sustainable food system. Business leaders act on facts and are often the best to translate global risks into business opportunities. The demand for healthier and more sustainably produced foods will continue to rise and bring about exciting business opportunities for the forward-thinking companies. It is starting to happen and companies are beginning to understand that there are opportunities for innovation and profitmaking. EAT is a one-of-a-kind forum where we aspire to create a place to enable this sort of dialogue, where leaders from civil society, policymakers, the scientific community, academia and businesses can collectively create a win–win–win path to a healthy, sustainable global food system.

Understandably, food is one of the last remaining cultural taboos. Food is deeply rooted in people's history, culture, religions, and traditions. Exacerbating this challenge is the fact that people don't want to be told what to eat. In addition, the drivers of eating behavior must be acknowledged: price, taste, and availability. Hence, to change diets at the level of populations, healthy and sustainable foods must be competitive against unhealthy and less sustainable alternatives. In addition, we need to help people discover ways to honor their cultures and traditions while having healthy, sustainable diets that enable generations to come to thrive.

Discoveries and learnings along the way

Interestingly, the force of capitalism might be the only force strong enough to create the required changes quickly enough to enable us to collectively transform the global food system. To enable businesses to operate more sustainably and profit on the business opportunities that evolve in the food–health–sustainability nexus, a closely coordinated multi-stakeholder effort is needed. There is no doubt that tremendous business opportunities will arrive along the path to a sustainable, healthy global food system.

The most important and meaningful lesson I have learned on my journey so far has arisen out of my bout with systemic scleroderma. I used to think I had 50 years to make a difference in the world. All of a sudden, because my prognosis was so poor, I had to ask myself: how much change can I accomplish in *one year*? I will keep that one-year perspective, no matter how long I live. I have learned that we cannot take for granted that we have a lifetime to fulfill our dreams because that leads to the question: what is a lifetime? We have to act now!

What I learned from Gunhild Stordalen

Gunhild is without question *the* most visionary, committed person I have met on my 20-year quest spotlighting DreamMakers. She has the courage to envision a flourishing world and the extraordinary commitment to authentically dedicate her life to making that dream come true against tremendous obstacles. It is DreamMakers like Gunhild Stordalen that have inspired humanity over the course of the history of humankind to strive for a positive future. Her compelling vision has the potential to bring us together so we can find the strength and the love to finally rise out of our parochial views of life and co-create a healthy, beautiful, sustainable world.

The following are Gunhild's opening remarks at the EAT Stockholm Food Forum, 2015. I was personally inspired and touched by her words and I want to share them with you verbatim:

> I know that one day we will have complete knowledge of the complex interactions between food, health and the environment, we will have integrated guidelines for healthy diets from sustainable food systems, we will have global and local policies with effective incentives to ensure public adherence to these guidelines. And the most thriving and successful companies will be the ones selling genuine happy meals, where "happy" is not the throw away toy at the bottom of the box, but the creation of shared values along the entire value chain; happy cows, happy communities, happy and healthy customers. This is the promised land. In our imaginations, in research labs, in business plans, in political manifestos, we are already there. Unfortunately, there is an existing gap between theory and practice; we will bridge that gap, it is not a question of if, but when. With the steady progress we see across the world, I'm confident it will be soon, but with the remaining challenges we still face, let's make sure it is soon enough.
>
> Today thanks to agricultural and technological innovations, we are feeding more people than ever. At the same time, current food production causes major environmental challenges, threatening current food security, it drives climate change, threatening future food security. The striking contrast between the starving and the obese is

alarming and for the first time, unhealthy diets kill more than smoking.

When more under- and over-nutrition and micronutrient deficiencies are taken together, as much as half the global population is classified as malnourished, and half of what we produce never gets eaten. Never before have so many children survived the age of 5, yet never before are so many kids destined for a lifetime with diabetes before the age of 9.

We need to invest more in prevention, not simply better drugs. Prevention is a much better strategy than treatment, for our health, for the environment and for society's wallets.

But transforming the global food system is a huge task. We need structural mechanisms to enable individual efforts, so that the world's 7 billion people, more than 9 billion by 2050 all can make a small positive change, each time they sit down to eat.

I used to imagine I had a lifetime to make a difference. I just forgot that one crucial question, what is a lifetime? When we met here last May, I used to think I had at least another 50 years to make the world a better place, but half a year ago, all of a sudden, I had to ask myself: How much positive change can I create in only one year? And for those of you wondering, I did not pick this haircut by choice, let's just say I traded my ponytail in for new bone marrow.

For a long time, much like we all have chosen to ignore clear signs that our ecosystems are reaching fatal tipping points. I myself had refused to admit that my own body was turning into my worst enemy. [In October 2014] I was diagnosed with a life-threatening autoimmune disease. Five years ago a cure for this disease was not even heard of, and that's why someone said, my even being here today is a bit of a wonder. I say it's the result of two things: persistent goals and scientific breakthroughs. Indeed, thanks to this I am living proof that whatever seems incurable or unimaginable does not have to be impossible.

So far my experiential treatment has been successful and my life expectancy is more or less back to normal and looking back I am pretty much the same person I use to be, except one thing, I have kept that one-year perspective!

And here is my take home message; if there is one year to create positive change that will dramatically influence generations to come, 2015 is the year. 2015 is a window of global opportunities we cannot let pass by. 2015 is the year the UN defines its new Sustainable Development Goals; 2015 is the year leaders will meet in Paris to agree upon the binding CO_2 emission targets and 2015 could be the year several of our eco systems reach their tipping points. So let's figure out how we, in the coming one-year period, can create opportunities for a lifetime.

To get there, the promised land, we need new tools and indicators; we need an integrated framework and we need tangible targets, and as you all agree, we need more data. But we must also challenge existing business models all along the value chain. A central engine in this shift will inevitably be the food industry itself, guided by politicians willing to look further than their own office terms, and driven by new demands and emerging markets, created by new affluent and conscious consumers, Taken together, this will pave the way for the triple bottom line; people, planet and profits, to become reality.

Today's main bottlenecks are not lack of knowledge, finances or political will, the main obstacles are lack of coordination, cooperation and co-creation. EAT is not the solution, EAT is a model for co-creating solutions. EAT is a catalytic hub, merging the disciplines of food health and sustainability across science, business and politics. Everyone in this room represents great visions and achievements within their fields of expertise. You might be a Nobel Prize Laureate or a nerdy guy with a wild idea waiting to be realized. Some of you are heads of states, some of you are senior advisors with a lifelong dedication to your work; you might be a CEO of a multinational industrial conglomerate or running a groundbreaking startup out in the Swedish countryside.

Individually your contribution might affect lunch time at the local school in Emuel, a restaurant menu in Kuala Lumpur, a fish tank in Chile or a board meeting at the United Nations. Together, together, you can transform knowledge into action for a whole generation, and the next to come; because if you can't who can, and if this is not the time and place, tell me where and when?

Rid-All cofounders, Damien Forshe, Keymah Durden and Randy McShepard

9
Rid-All: green in the ghetto

RID ALL
GREEN PARTNERSHIP
Urban Agriculture and Youth Education

"Redeem, Integrity, Determination for ALL mankind"

I first learned about Rid-All from Rich Cochran, CEO of Western Reserve Land Conservancy. I visited the campus in 2013 hosted by Rich who had invited me on an "Urban Immersion" tour to see first-hand the renaissance that was occurring in Cleveland. Rid-All became the centerpiece of that visit. I have become a huge fan and a tireless cheerleader of this very special place and these very special men.

Rid-All Green Partnership is the dream of three closely knit childhood friends, Damien Forshe, Keymah Durden, and Randy McShepard, who grew up together in Cleveland's Lee-Miles neighborhood, also known as "the Forgotten Triangle." They have reclaimed 3 acres of abandoned land and transformed it into a flourishing urban farm, a unique learning center, and a thriving enterprise that provides healthy local food to area companies, institutions, and the community. They train others in urban farming and environmental stewardship and Rid-All is a Regional Training

FIGURE 9.1   Rid-All greenhouses

FIGURE 9.2   Rid-All fish farming

FIGURE 9.3 "Black gold"

Center for Growing Power, the Milwaukee-based urban farm founded by Will Allen, the godfather of urban agriculture.

These social entrepreneurs have constructed three green houses, four hoop houses and developed an edible trail and a pond. They have planted 18 trees and they have even built a tree house and a teepee. They are growing fruits and vegetables, farming fish and creating and selling rich nutritious soil that they call "black gold" (see Figs. 9.1, 9.2, 9.3 and 9.6).

> We are raising tasty tilapia fish in our four large tanks. So far we've sold more than 350 pounds of the omega-3-packed fish raised in our aquaponic system that cleans and recirculates water between our fish tanks and vegetables growing on the roof.
>
> ...
>
> We take food waste add some worms and make "black gold," a rich nutritious soil. It's ideal for farms, roof-top gardens and raised-bed gardens in inner-city neighborhoods where people are concerned about digging in the ground. This is the soil in which we grow our vegetables (Rid-All Green Partnership website).

Alongside its educational program Rid-All offers a host of art, entertainment, sports, and community engagement programs. It sells organic clothing designed by Marc White who has designed clothes for Oprah Winfrey, Wynton Marsalis, and Whitney Houston. His Reconstructed Gear is made from sustainable materials such as hemp, linen, and bamboo. Rid-All even has a mindfulness practice to nurture the spirit.

Rid-All has reached hundreds of kids with a comic book series and a coloring book for young ones. It is sponsored by Cleveland businesses, nonprofits, and foundations. The *Brink City "Green in the Ghetto"* comic book was created to communicate the importance of the green movement and environmental justice to non-traditional and hard-to-reach audiences, with a particular emphasis on urban youth. The stories in the series promote positive messages that highlight urban agriculture, recycling, green jobs, safety, and neighborhood pride, which are all key components for healthy families and communities (see Fig. 9.4).

FIGURE 9.4 *Brink City "Green in the Ghetto"* comic book series

FIGURE 9.5   Rid-All Green Partnership Anti-Gun-Violence Art Competition

> We are working with local schools and sponsoring an essay contest to encourage students to understand the effect "woes" have in the community. Those woes include contaminated water and soil—including the land Rid-All has transformed into a healthy, flouring urban farm (Damien Forshe).

One of the most compelling and thought-provoking programs Rid-All has offered is its gun buy-back initiative. On the day of the interview for this book, Damien took me on a tour of the campus; it was flourishing with fruits and vegetables and bustling with people. I was very impressed. We ended up at the Rid-All teepee. When we walked inside there was a fascinating art exhibit that displayed sculptures and paintings from young people who had participated in Rid-All's Anti-Gun-Violence Art Competition (Fig. 9.5). The exhibit was the result of their toy gun buy-back program where they invited parents in the community to bring their children to turn in their toy guns. In return they received $25 and a special edition of the Rid-All comic book *Brink City, Kids Lives Matter*.

We had talked about a gun buy-back program. It was something we always had in our mind but all came together when one of our partners, Fred Ward, founder of the Khnemu Foundation, a community center on the Eastside of Cleveland. saw a young child playing with a toy gun over near his center. Fred offered him our *Brink City* comic books in exchange for the toy gun; the boy happily agreed. That gave form to the idea, so we started talking about doing an official toy buy-back event. We were still talking about when Tamier Rice, an unarmed 12-year-old boy was killed by the police, for carrying what turned out to be a toy gun here in Cleveland. After that we decided it was time to launch the program. We held two toy gun buy-backs in collaboration with some serious community partners: Cleveland Police Foundation, InnerVisions. The Gloria Pointer Foundation, Dave's Supermarket, the Policy Bridge, and the Boys and Girls Club. We collected 125 toy guns. We decided to turn the toy guns into artwork by inviting local artist to express their creativity using the toy guns we collected. We decided to transform them from instruments of violence into instruments of peace and creativity (Keymah Durden, Rid-All).

It's amazing how Rid-All has evolved. It was "Godly led"; we were pointed in this direction. I would have never thought I would be doing this work (Damien Forshe).

FIGURE 9.6   Rid-All teepee: "a place for tranquility"

I sat with the founders and two of their colleagues in a circle in front of their teepee and listened to the fascinating stories that led them to co-create Rid-All. It was an appropriate setting to reflect on what sounded like a spiritual quest. Each of their stories seemed to be tributaries flowing into one powerful, fast-moving river of love. I am inspired, proud, and thankful for the contribution these amazing men are making in the lives of so many living in urban communities. I am hopeful that their vision will help change the inner and outer landscape of urban America.

These men have a unique organic relationship; there is no hierarchy or even a traditional approach to collaboration. Everyone brings his expertise to the table, they complement each other, and everyone lends his gifts naturally. Some people say you should never mix friendship and business; these wonderful men contradict that "should-ism." Each of these guys has followed his own path and yet stayed connected, and now they have come together to co-create their life's mission. It is my pleasure to introduce you to G. Keymah Durden III, Damien Forshe, Randy McShepard, Marc White, and Dave Hester.

Meet the Rid-All cofounders

Highest aspirations for Rid-All

Keymah. Let me take a step back and set a context for our vision. The local food market in urban cities across America is one of the most underserved sectors in society. What communities are able to grow on a local level barely makes a dent in the foods that come into local cities. Our biggest aspiration is to see as many people create as many local farms as possible. People in low-income communities are suffering; their health is bad and their access to healthy food either very limited or nonexistent. The more projects like Rid-All that exist throughout the country, the more access people will have to fresh, healthy foods. This will enable people to dramatically improve their quality of life. We see this as a movement, a renaissance. We are teaching people how to plant, grow, and maintain healthy gardens in the smallest amount of space with healthy soil and clean water.

Damien. We want to feed knowledge, food, health, and wellness to people in communities in urban cites around the country; we want to replicate the Rid-All model. We have already replicated our model in Columbus, Ohio, at St. Stevens Community House, one of the oldest settlement houses in the country. They care for over 90,000 residents in the low-income area of the city. We trained 12 of their employees and helped them build a site. Today they have a fish farm, a compost facility, and a greenhouse and they even have a teepee for the tranquility. We are on track to replicate two to three major projects per year.

Randy. We think that Rid-All is a blueprint for urban America. Every urban city is dealing with vacant land, high unemployment, community disinvestment, a waning sense of pride and disconnectedness. We believe that our farm is a great example of how you can repurpose vacant land, bring communities back together, create jobs, and make more productive, inclusive, safer communities all over America.

In my vision I see a big movement. There will be a healthy buzz around the city. People will be excited to be growing their own gardens and buying fresh produce from not only our site, but similar sites across the city and across the country. People will be a lot more health-conscious and there would be a lot less health disparity. We will see dramatically decreasing health problems like high blood pressure and obesity. Kids will be talking about what it feels like to put their hands in the soil. They will understand that vegetables come from gardens, not the grocery store. People will also feel a sense of accomplishment and a sense of community.

Core values

Randy. Our core values are the foundation of this movement. **Empowerment**, because it is all about giving people the power to take back their lives and neighborhoods. **Community**—this is not about us at Rid-All or a business or a garden—it is about bringing people together. **Love**—we love each other, we love the community, we know that these communities don't have enough love. Love nurtures and enables people and communities to flourish.

Defining moments

Keymah. We all grew up together, we had a shared experience in our childhood. We joined each other's families and friends, we were one. Cleveland historically was a steel town so our families came out of that environment. We came from blue-collar, middle-class working families from the southeast side of Cleveland. At a young age we learned very strong work ethics. One of our first businesses was shoveling snow and cutting grass together. We learned those skills from Dave and his grandparents. They taught us the value of earning money and developing resources at a young age. We had good role models coming up and we have become each other's role models too. We all have defined a unique lane and a unique space within our organization. Everyone on the team is a master at what they do. We are doing our life's purpose. When you get in-purpose, everything flows, that's how you know you've hit your stride.

After graduation Damien and I went to Kent State together, that's where we met Marc. Towards the latter part of our experience at Kent we had what I guess you would call a spiritual awakening. We became curious about our history, our Black culture. Kent State is historically known for having a very strong Pan-African Department so a lot of people who came through Kent became culturally conscious. So we started exploring the bible and there were no Africans, no Blacks in the bible, so we went on a journey in search of our spirituality to discover who we were and how we connected to this bigger picture called life. Marc graduated and moved to Washington, DC, and then moved to Israel. I stayed in the US and worked for corporate America for about five years and then I decided to leave corporate and go out on my own. I started a vegetarian restaurant here in Cleveland in the mid-1990s called Soul Vegetarian and expanded into an international chain with restaurants in Atlanta, Chicago, Washington, DC, Ghana, West Africa, and Israel. All the while, I stayed in contact these guys.

Then about seven years ago I became more green conscious. We were doing some green projects in Israel and I was traveling back and forth to visit with Marc. We became passionate about the earth because it fits into our spiritual paradigm—certainly if you love people and you love God, you naturally love nature and being healthy. So I went back to school to learn about being green and earned a postgraduate certificate in environmental studies. That's when we started talking about creating Rid-All Green Partnership. We went to Milwaukee and met with Will Allen, founder and CEO of Growing Power Inc. He is recognized as a preeminent practitioner of urban agriculture in America and throughout the world. We cannot have a legitimate conversation about the defining moments in the development of Rid-All without talking about Will Allen; we modeled Rid-All after what we learned from him.

Damien. My story starts when I was six or seven years old. My older cousin Dave would come over everyday and educate us on recycling and the environment. He would tell us: "don't step on the plants, don't litter." He was very conscious even back then. When we were kids, Keymah, Randy and I were very close. We worked and played together everyday. We also participated in skating and dancing talent shows. We would be at my house or Randy's house almost every day.

I was the youngest so when they went off to college I missed them so much. While they were away, I was out on the streets, getting into all kinds of things I shouldn't have. I was trying to figure life out. I tried different kinds of jobs and it was just not working. I learned early on that I did not want to work for anyone. So I decided to get my mind together to create my own business. So in 1994, I got a job with Orkin as an exterminator. They had a contract with public housing and they had to hire some minorities to fulfill their contract. At first the experience was a nightmare. I had dreams for about a month about cockroaches all over me because the public housing was terrible; the units were out of control in 1995. As I got to know the people in the housing complexes I started feeling more compassionate and more conscious of their needs. I started trying to figure out ways to help. So I started my own exterminating company because I wanted to create a black corporation that could help the community.

I ended up leveraging the Rid-All name as an umbrella organization to launch Rid-All Green Partnership: Redeem—to free from what distresses or harms; Integrity—adherence to moral and ethical principles, soundness of moral character, honest; Determination—the act of coming to a decision or of fixing or settling a purpose; for *All* mankind.

While I was growing my business I came back in contact with my older cousin Dave who had left Cleveland. I really missed him. When we were kids he spent a lot of time with us; he taught us karate, he took us to see Muhammad Ali and he taught us about nature. When our uncle died Dave told me he was leaving Cleveland because he needed a job. I was devastated, so I asked him how I could help. I offered him a job and he came to work at Rid-All. Then I remembered from my childhood that his passion was nature, gardening, and what we now call sustainability so I decided to build him a greenhouse. I was always conscious of valuing nature but I really did not know how it was all going to come together, especially since I had been an exterminator dealing in pest control using harmful chemicals.

After Dave came to work at Rid-All we would sit at his house, what we called the Think Tank, discussing how we were going to move the business to the next level. Then one day Dave and I met a young woman named Evelyn Burnett and she told us about getting into the green space. Then and there, I decided to make myself a green exterminating company and we made it happen.

That just goes to show you what you can do when you put your mind to it. I started sharing natural solutions: 100% peppermint oil, for example, will get rid of mice. Hot sauce will get rid of roaches. We used natural, organic solutions rather than using harmful chemicals. What I really discovered about the green space boils down to food, "He who feeds is who leads."

When Dave and Keymah came back to the table we realized it was about sustainable food. So Evelyn introduced us to Will Allen and together we made Rid-All Green Partnership happen. We went to Milwaukee on the coldest day I can ever remember. Will took us into a greenhouse and it was 70 degrees. We learned you can heat a greenhouse without electricity through a process called "Hotmix," mixing beer hops, coffee grounds, and wood chips together to create natural heat. When he took us into the fish farm and showed us the fish, I was sold. Once Will figured out that we were committed he let us into his training program—that was in 2010. We had to go to Milwaukee one weekend a month for five months. I remember at one of the classes we were asked to draw our vision and Dave drew the Rid-All Partnership campus exactly as it looks today.

We started planning how we would acquire land and get the project moving. Since I had a business I put up the initial money and we started moving forward. When we approached graduation Will Allen asked me, "would you be interested in becoming one of my ROTCs?" I told him I didn't want to join the military (there was an army base right next to his center). Will laughed and said 'No, I mean a Regional Outreach Training Center for the country … you guys are doing so well I would like you to represent our ROTCs across the country." That's how it all got started. But truth be told, I did all this because I really missed my family—Keymah, Randy, Dave, and Marc. Rid-All was actually a trick to lure them back home to me. My whole mission, my passion is fed by being around my family and seeing them every day. These guys are my family.

Randy. I grew up in a single parent household; my mother raised three of us. I saw how hard she worked to take care of us. I didn't see her much because she always worked two jobs. I think that was when I had my first Aha! moment and decided to take personal responsibility to ease her burden. A lot of people in my neighborhood were doing the wrong things but I had clear direction from my mother about the kind of person she wanted me to become. She was forced to leave me to my own devices quite a bit so I started working when I was 12. I worked during the summers and saved all my money. I bought all my school clothes and that gave my mother one less thing to worry about. I think that carried over to my adult work life. I often tell the story that I have worked the last 25 years without calling in sick and I think it's because I never saw my mom call in sick. There were days she didn't feel well but she showed me that you just get up and do what you have to do.

Another big defining moment was my first job out of college. I worked for an agency that helped disabled and disadvantaged populations, primarily with job training and job placement assistance. These were people who had dropped out of high school, dislocated workers, welfare moms, people released from prison, and people with disabilities. It was there that I realized that I had a real gift for writing. I started winning all these grant proposals. As a young twenty-something, I remember thinking, "wow, I'm a really powerful guy. I can dream up an idea for a program, put pen to paper and people will give me large amounts of money to go make the program happen." At one point I had four federal grants, a budget of 1.4 million dollars, 15 people working for me and it was all because I would dream up ideas of better ways we could help this population. It blossomed; it was amazing to see the impact I could make as such a young guy. I remember thinking to myself, "there aren't many African American men in the social services that would sacrifice making less money, to make a difference in other people's lives." I was proud to see so many people's lives change. People would bring their families down to meet me and say, "This is the man that helped me put my family back together by helping me get a job." So I feel today that everyone can do something to make a difference and since this is a gift I have been given, I need to use it wisely and try to help people when and where I can.

My journey to Rid-All started with a think tank I cofounded called PolicyBridge. I led the work to establish research for a report that was titled *Rebuilding Blocks*. It was focused on getting to the truth about the disinvesting in urban neighborhoods, which the media was blaming on the foreclosure crisis. I knew that was not true; disinvestment in urban communities had been happening for decades, the foreclosure crisis was just the tipping point that helped the bottom to fall out. I felt someone needed to tell this story so I started researching and writing. At the end of that report we made recommendations and one of them was to amass and repurpose vacant land and transform it into urban farms and gardens. This would help forgotten, disinvested neighborhoods to see a rebirth in their communities. It would also create jobs, improve health, and improve the overall quality of life in these neighborhoods. Damien and Keymah read the report and said, "That's it, this is the blueprint, this is what we need to do." Keymah was already a vegan with vegetarian restaurants and had already laid down the path to healthy eating. We knew this was something that could really benefit people and that we were living in a food desert. Damien knew how to get the permits to start building greenhouses right away.

This is how God really works. I often find myself in the middle of being a connector of some sort. The city of Cleveland had its first sustainability summit in 2009. There was a young African American woman named Evelyn Burnett who was organizing and coordinating the summit and she was having problems finding minorities to register. Around that same time there were two guys that had an urban hip hop radio show called Green in the Ghetto. They would do a 10-minute segment on "going green" in a real hip, comical way. They came to me and asked me to help them to be taken more seriously by the radio station. Their real goal was to find a corporate sponsor to back their sustainability segment. I approached Damien and he agreed to sponsor their segment for a month. I then suggested they invite Evelyn to come on their show and talk about the sustainability summit. Evelyn came to me looking for help, these hip hop radio guys came to me looking for help and I introduced them to each other. I then took Evelyn and the two hip hop guys to meet Damien because we were all in this green space, and it was in that meeting that Evelyn said, "If you guys are serious about urban farming you need to hook up with Will Allen, the godfather of urban farming." So we all went to Milwaukee to meet with Will Allen and things started to flow.

Another defining moment, a part of the flow, was the evolution of our comic book series *Brink City "Green in the Ghetto,"* with a tagline that comes from the two hip hop radio show guys. The artist was an employee of Damien's, Martinez E-B Garcia, and we all got together and decided to collaborate on the creation of the comic book series. *Brink City*—meaning a city on the brink of disaster. The characters in the comic book are real everyday people in the community that looked like them and it was created in a hip way, rather than having a judgmental approach where you lectured kids to eat their fruit and vegetables. The artist made all of us characters in the book. Keymah is Veggie Man, I'm Info Man, always trying to connect everyone, and Dave is Dr. Greenhand.

We had another great opportunity. I was a former board member of the Sisters of Charity Health Systems Foundation, a group of nuns that came to Cleveland 150 years ago. They started schools and a couple of hospitals. They sold some of their hospitals and used the proceeds to fund conversion projects where you could convert old businesses for charitable purposes. They started giving money from their endowment for that purpose. I had served on the board of directors for nine years and I was chairman of the board for my last two years. Sister Judith Ann was the lead administrator for their network of facilities. She was a very powerful woman. The neighborhood where our farm is located was where their first hospital was built, so they had a soft spot in their heart for that community. They were launching programs on healthy eating, nutrition, and exercise, so Sister Judith Ann sat me down and asked "Randy, how can I help?" I said, "You run a hospital that serves fruits and vegetables 365 days a year. If you will commit to buying 5% of them from Rid-All, it would be a game-changer, we would immediately have serious clientele." So she set up a meeting with Sudexo, the corporate business that supplied their fruits and vegetables, we brought in Will Allen and they committed to source from Rid-All. We were not big enough to provide all they needed so we set up our first co-op where we buy vegetables from other local farmers. So many farmers benefited, it was win–win–win for everyone. So we did that coming out of the gate with Rid-All. We were still figuring out how this all would work. We received our equivalent to a PhD in food handling, refrigeration, packaging, pricing, staffing, and all the components of the business. That catapulted us forward; it was a very successful collaboration. It took off from there, everyone found their lane and it blossomed. It has been fun and funny to watch.

We have this culturally relevant urban farm that ties composting, urban farming, and aquaponics together. We are the only level 2 composting operation and the only fish farming company in the city of Cleveland. It is amazing how everything flows when you are on your path.

Marc. I feel blessed being here. As a fashion designer, my whole segway into greening has to do with health and beauty from the inside out. I come from the belief that we are an outer reflection of our inner condition. What goes on inside of an individual usually radiates on the outside of them and that is a testimony to their confidence. You can tell how a person is feeling from their aura, the vibe when you come upon them. No matter what is in style or in fashion, the human body will always be the most fashionable, the most beautiful, and the most reflective of God's creation. So I thought that was an excellent niche for me within the context of fashion.

I spend most of my life developing ways to assist and enhance the human body and the human spirit: "I bless you then I dress you." I have a degree in fashion design from Kent State; I was the first African American to graduate from that program. I was always into fashion. When I was a little kid, 12 or 13 years old, I used to alter and style my clothes. My parents were educators and administrators on the school board. My father was the department chairman for Industrial Arts. My mother was a professor of Business Administration. I lost my mom when I was 11 and that created a big void in my life, the void of the nurturer. I think that is why I was always searching for that beauty. That's what mom represents, that hug, the meals, Christmas; that's why I cherish beauty. That's why I believe we can always find that beauty in nature and find a way to mimic what God has given us in textures, patterns and colors.

I have been doing this work since I was 16 years old. I lived abroad for 21 years, mainly in Israel and parts of West Africa. When I was a child my father told me we were from Israel. I didn't know what he meant by that, or how it was all connected so I went to search for the truth. As a young man soon out of college I was blessed to have acquired many clients: Wynton Marsalis, Oprah Winfrey, Spike Lee. I was designing for a lot of famous entertainers. So I was able to maintain my life as a freelance designer and entrepreneur. I was 22 years old at the time and I had achieved what many called success; however, I want something more. I wanted to search for my truth. So I went on this journey to understand my real self. I became a humanitarian in search of how we can restore our humanity. I was involved in organizations that dug wells in Ghana. I had a place in Accra where the American Embassy is located. I really fell in love with helping people. I married and had eight children that I raised in Israel. I met my wife in Israel, but she is from Cleveland; that's why I believe in providence. I went all the way to Israel to meet a girl from Cleveland. We lived in Dimona, near where the Dead Sea scrolls were discovered.

These guys brought me back to Cleveland. We never broke contact, especially Keymah and I; not a month went by over the last twenty-something years when we did not talk with one another. All of our lives' endeavors were interwoven. Rid-All Green Partnerships is naturally a reflection of a project I was doing in Israel. This is how we live and breathe. If you are going to try to live in a way that's sustainable, your life must be a testimony to that. The older you get the more you try to tweak, hone and refine that process. We inspire each other; I get inspired by these guys every day in many, many ways. It goes without saying that we have an organic relationship. No one dictates roles or what needs to happen, the spirit dictates our actions.

Dave, Dr. Greenhand. I have been "in-purpose" since I was five years old; I already knew what I was supposed to do. My true passion came from my grandmother. She taught me that all great conversations are around a meal. She grew her own food and there were a lot of us born around the same time. She had 50 grandchildren and she took care of her mother at the same time so she needed to give us something to do. You were either going to pick some seeds, do some watering, or do some weeding; working in her garden kept us in line. I would watch her as she would talk to the plants. She was so protective of them. I remember thinking, what is it about them that she loves them so much? Then I began to understand; she was producing food and beauty and people were happy because her yard was so beautiful. When we were in elementary school we always won the biggest ribbons from the 4-H Club. I learned from my grandmother that the secret to beautiful, healthy plants and vegetables is the soil and clean water. Soil is alive. The definition healthy soil is that is viable, it has nutrients and plants are able to live in grow in it. There is a whole ecosystem within that living soil. In dirt you only have mud, dust particles, and a little bit of soil; it is inert—it is not alive.

So as a teenager I was focused on landscaping and one day my father told me, "the lawn looks great, but I know you want to eat, so you need to come help me in the backyard." That's when I got into growing vegetables and I loved it. When I was 16, in 1975, they closed the horticulture program at my high school. I was devastated! That was my career path they were taking away. I decided to go to Ohio State but I got into a little bit of trouble so I ended up going into the military to get the GI Bill. I ended up going overseas and learned about farming in Japan and Brazil. My mother got sick while I was on tour in Washington, DC, so I came home and I decided it was time for me to take care of her. I had left when I was 16 and returned when I was 32; it was time and I had learned a lot. When she recovered I planned to go back to DC where I could work in my field, but that's when Damien offered me a job at his exterminating company.

We would go into apartments and see what they were eating. There were noodles and stuff, but no fruits or vegetables. It saddened me so much; there was a sense of hopelessness there. People thought this how they were supposed to live. Both of my parents died from diabetes and that could have been prevented because it was directly related to food. That really pushed me to further pursue this mission. We lost a lot of family members and friends from preventable diseases due to their diet.

Greatest obstacle

The group. Negative energy is always the greatest obstacle. When people bring negative energy we overcome it by showing them love. Positive always overcomes negative. This is a soft place to land. Most people that come here feel the living spirit here and we want to keep it that way. Anyone can build a hoop house or a greenhouse, but it is really about the spirit people feel when they are here.

Greatest lessons learned: a powerful group discussion on "momentum"

Never burn bridges. If you truly try to help everyone along your life's path there will be sweet returns; people will be just as eager to help you.

Adversity is never a thing we should run from. Adversity prepares you for opportunities down the road that you just don't see when you are going through it. Adversity is coming; it's all about how you handle it.

We all keep the mission and the vision going no matter what. We want the world to be a better place. So when you find a group of brothers that share this vision you can't help but resonate and become one with that. Part of the problem with many humans is that we are so busy trying to find ways to segment and divide, as opposed to unite. So much energy is spent on separating.

We were young when we started together and everyone went off and did their own thing. Then our spirit and our purpose naturally pulled us back together. The secret sauce is our relationship, our love. We just used the "Disney World" of agriculture to wake up the other people. If you are around here, you will feel it. That's what we mean by "the natural effect." I've watched people just cry when they come here. Whatever you need to get, we allow you to get it here, but love is the key—if you have love in your heart you will move forward.

Keymah. I will leave you with a thought: it is important not only for this project but for anything important. It is one thing to start something but is another thing to keep it going. One of the key ingredients to sustaining momentum is innovation. Continuing to create and push the envelope. Keep asking, "What is possible?" We stay innovative and we keep dreaming of what is possible to create in an urban space. For example, who builds a teepee in the inner city? We keep reintroducing energy. The way you sustain that momentum is by infusing that energy so the secret is innovation.

Having a group of people around you that pushes you is also critical, that is why this social innovation we have created is so important. African American children that come here on field trips are full of pride. They have never been on a field trip to a place owned by African American men. They see our passion, our compassion, and our love. Rid-All is the canvas that keeps our imagination alive. It has allowed us to paint a new reality and show people living in forgotten communities in urban cities what is possible.

What I learned from the Rid-All cofounders

These men are on a heartfelt mission. They epitomize the power of shared vision and values and the role that powerful, positive relationships play in transforming dreams into reality. I experienced a place full of love, peace, and possibility. Everything and everyone was in harmony, rooted in these courageous men's vision of healthy urban communities. There was something else that I experienced that is rare and somewhat unfamiliar in public places; I felt a sense of spirit at play. These men are consciously guided by a sacred energy that manifests itself in every aspect of the Rid-All campus. If you want to feel love go visit this precious place and meet these amazing men.

Rich Cochran, President and CEO,
Western Reserve Land Conservancy

10
Western Reserve Land Conservancy: from vacancy to vitality

We provide the people of our region with natural assets through land conservation and restoration. When our work is done, our region will be filled with thriving, prosperous communities nourished by vibrant natural areas, working farms and healthy cities (Rich Cochran, President and CEO, Western Reserve Land Conservancy).

I'd like to introduce you to Rich Cochran, President and CEO, Western Reserve Land Conservancy. Rich is what I call a practical visionary. Although his vision of people and the planet harmoniously flourishing is as big and bold as any leader, his focus is on rolling up his sleeves and making it happen. I met Rich through David Cooperrider, cofounder of Appreciative Inquiry and founder of the Fowler Center for Business as an Agent of World Benefit. I sit on David's advisory board and in 2013 he had invited me to attend Cleveland's summit on Sustainable Cleveland 2019. The summit was initiated by Mayor Frank Jackson in 2009. Each year Mayor Jackson brings hundreds of people together from across sectors, disciplines, and neighborhoods to collaborate, share information and plan ways to transform their city from what was once known as "the mistake on the lake" into their shared vision of a "thriving green city on a blue lake." I was there to write a piece in the *Huffington Post* about Cleveland's big, bold vision and the city-wide collaborative process. The place was buzzing with excitement, people sharing their stories and networking.

When Rich began to talk about the mission of Western Reserve Land Conservancy it was immediately apparent that he was passionately committed to the work and proud of his organization's accomplishments. When you see and feel that kind of passion and enthusiasm you can't help but stop and listen. I discovered that Rich leads one of the most impactful conservation organizations in the United States. Its highly collaborative, holistic approach has brought it national recognition for the tremendous impact and scope of its work. It has preserved nearly 50,000 acres of land in 23 counties, which has had a tremendous positive effect on the environment and the communities of northeast Ohio. It has permanently preserved meadows, streams, wetlands, forests, camps, parks, and family farms, enabling flora and fauna to flourish. In partnership with its communities, it is co-creating "thriving, prosperous communities nourished by vibrant natural lands, working farms and healthy cities." I was impressed. In light of the severe environmental crisis our planet is facing, Western Reserve Land Conservancy gives me hope. Here is living proof that we humans have the capacity to restore and renew our environment.

On my ride through the city en route to the airport my hope began to fade. I saw and felt the degradation of the inner city; boarded up vacant homes, neighborhoods that looked like ghost towns, and people that appeared helpless and hopeless. I could physically feel my energy and optimism wane. I remember wondering how was it possible to have flourishing suburbs and countryside brushing against crumbling cities. It defied logic. Our man-made boundaries can't actually compartmentalize the ecosystem because air, water, and people naturally flow and will either contaminate or nurture the whole. I returned home still somewhat optimistic about Cleveland's vision of a "thriving green city on a blue lake" and impressed by the phenomenal progress Western Reserve Land Conservancy had made towards preserving and renewing the countryside. I was disheartened, however, by the gap between Cleveland's vision for 2019 and the city's deteriorating neighborhoods and the dichotomy between the flourishing countryside and those deteriorating neighborhoods. This is a common dilemma we face around the world.

I had been home a couple of days when I received an email from Rich inviting me to come back to Cleveland for what he called an "urban revitalization immersion." I was curious and perplexed. Why was Rich inviting me to spend two days immersed in Cleveland's neighborhoods? Well the truth is, I had allowed my stereotypical view of nature conservancies to cloud my understanding of the breadth and depth of Western Reserve Land Conservancy's mission and work. I had wrongly interpreted "thriving communities" to mean towns and villages in the suburbs and countryside. This assumption was completely shattered during my two-day immersion into Western Reserve Land Conservancy's brand of urban revitalization. Its Thriving Communities initiative is "helping cities across Ohio to go from vacancy to vitality." In collaboration with local grassroots community leaders and local governments the initiative is creating some very innovative solutions to deeply rooted problems. The results have been extraordinary; Rich and his team of urban planners, biologists, lawyers, communicators, real-estate professionals, fundraisers, and public policy experts bring people and resources together to help revitalize cities throughout Ohio that have been devastated by the foreclosure crisis. They have led the effort to establish more than 30 new county land banks. They have raised $600 million since 2012 for urban revitalization, most of which went to removing abandoned homes in blighted neighborhoods and to begin the process of re-greening those areas. Partnering with community development corporations, municipal officials, residents, and grass-root organizations they launched Reforest Our City, an innovative program to restore the urban canopy. The greening strategies include an increased number of side yard lots and opportunities to work with city officials on the creation of parks and public green spaces. They also connect residents, community development corporations, block clubs, and churches

FIGURE 10.1   Community tree planting

with resources and knowledge that they need to clean and green their neighborhoods.

> The real heroes of the foreclosure crisis, are the residents with an empty side lot next to their property, a vacant boarded up house on the other side, and a house that's abandoned and open across the street. These residents get up in the morning, go to work, send their kids to school and confront these almost indescribable conditions every day. And yet they persist. They pay their taxes; they mow their yards; they fix the broken gutters and paint their homes. If they had done what the banks did, they would have packed everything into the trunk of their car and driven away. And fortunately for our city, they didn't. They're our first partner in the fight on blight (Jay Westbrook, special project manager for Western Reserve Land Conservancy's urban program, Thriving Communities).

The amazing part of this story, from my perspective, is that a regional land conservation organization that was founded in Hunting Valley, Ohio—one of the most affluent and racially uniform residential communities in America, home to a $70 million municipal endowment, countless millionaires, and several billion-aires—merged with 12 other land trusts from the region known as Northeast Ohio and as a part of their mission launched a major urban revitalization program in distressed cities such as Cleveland and Youngstown. This shattered the preconceived notion I held that conservation organizations, and most people living in the sub-urbs and countryside of Cleveland, were apathetic to the plight of the poor. It became clear to me that Rich's vision is holistic, that he understands how everything is connected, and that his organization had developed innovative, stereotype-shattering programs that make conservation an *essential* activity, rather than one that is simply "nice to have."

I sat down with Rich to talk about his vision, strategies and the important work they are doing in the urban neighborhoods. This was an extraordinary learning conversation; I had one aha! after another.

Meet Rich Cochran

Rich's vision

My vision for Western Reserve Land Conservancy is based on how people and communities thrive. It took me a long time to develop my vision because my thinking was limited by conventional thinking. In America we are raised to be prideful about individual efforts and consider that an individual's hard work and talent can overcome anything, and I grew up thinking that way. In the last ten years I have come to realize that such logic is flawed. All people and all communities are actually a reflection of their environment, not of some innate quality or gift. Certainly a person's talent and hard work influences their outcome, but they don't determine the outcome; their environment does.

I started working in the land conservation field in 1996. The Land Conservancy was a little land trust operating in the prosperous eastern suburbs of Cleveland in the Chagrin River Valley and I was the first employee. Over a ten-year period we grew a lot, becoming the largest land conservancy in Ohio. In 2006, we created Western Reserve Land Conservancy. It was the result of the largest-ever merger of land trusts in the United States. We merged eight land trusts that included 16 counties. During this time, I realized that our work is extremely important to the health and prosperity of people and communities; we were preserving a nutrient-rich environment. Nutrients meaning trees, clean air and clean water, scenic beauty, and farm soil. All of those things are positive for people and communities. They help places become enduring and prosperous and they attract people. That is when I started studying the big cities of the region to figure out how we could apply our vision, our values, our services, and our strengths to the cities.

When we did the merger we were aware that the cities of the region were losing population and that was contributing to urban sprawl. Most of the little land conservancies that merged were created to preserve land that was threatened by urban sprawl. I can remember one person saying, "why are we even bothering with the cities, they are not in our service areas?" I remember feeling a little frustrated and I said, "what we are doing right now feels like putting a Band-Aid on cancer." We were treating a symptom of a problem rather than its cause. The cause of urban sprawl was that the deteriorating conditions in the inner cities were pushing people out to the suburbs. We later realized that the people that were left behind were really in a very distressed environment. That is what created the environmental inequality that perpetuated and exacerbated the distress. The whole region was ultimately suffering from the fact that we had allowed our cities to deteriorate. People were running to the country. Whether they cared about the cities or not, everyone cared about the "push effect" that was driving urban sprawl. There was also a "pull effect": we were helping to beautify the country so people were not only being pushed out by the deteriorating conditions in the city, they were also pulled, or drawn, to the country by our investments in preserving a healthy and beautiful environment.

In 2011 we formed our urban program, Thriving Communities, which was designed to help revitalize Ohio's urban centers. We quickly realized that there is power in the cooperation between the whole system, urban and rural. It is one system, all interconnected. When we studied the cities, environmental quality came into our thinking. That's when the vision really evolved from just preserving foundational natural resources to realizing that urban environments had to be cleaned up first before they could be greened up. It didn't take long to realize that there was very little to preserve in the way of natural assets in some of the low-income neighborhoods in the cities. We had to create them. And before we could create them we had to get rid of the things that were perceived by people as toxins in their environments. Toxins are things like vacant homes that draw crime; gun shots are toxins; sirens of ambulances and police cars are toxins—it's all scary. We had to figure out how to address the foundational causes of those toxic things to help mitigate them. On the one hand, civic investment for the last 30 years has been great because it drove investment in our cities, but it has been flawed, on the other hand, because investment has often been too focused on massive civic amenities such as stadiums and downtown revitalizations, and not enough on cleaning up and greening residential communities that are distressed.

You have to do one with the other. It is a simple recipe: remove things people perceive as toxic and add things people perceive as nutrients. You can't have one without the other. Frankly a lot of that happened in Cleveland, which I am sure wasn't malevolent but rather an oversight. I always use Chester, Carnegie, and Euclid as examples. I call these avenues, or arteries, of illusion because I could drive from my beautiful little neighborhood in Shaker Heights, through the quaint neighborhood of Cedar Hill, down through University Circle and onto Chester, past the Cleveland Clinic to Cleveland Browns Stadium, and all I would see was hundreds of millions of dollars of investments. And at the stadium I'd be parked with a Mercedes on one side and a BMW on the other. So when my friend called me from Colorado and asked me, "how is Cleveland doing?" I would say great. But the reality is that 100 yards on either side of those arteries of illusion are terribly depressed neighborhoods. I did not know it, nor did anyone else living in Shaker Heights, because we never had a reason to be 100 yards off these avenues of illusion. I think it really set us back as a country. We isolated people from the brutal facts, people who could have done something about it. I think people are now realizing how extreme the situation is and many have the ability to help policy-wise or otherwise.

That is one of the powers of Western Reserve's urban programs: the policy work we have done. Due to the relationships and trust we have with elected officials at all levels of government, we have now raised about $600 million dollars in four years for urban revitalization. Our attorney general was responsible for bringing in the first $75 million. It was funded by one of the big settlements with banks. We convinced him there was a direct causal effect between the foreclosure crisis and the distress people have experienced, particularly in neighborhoods of Cleveland where we had mass abandonment of homes. Whole neighborhoods were decimated by the foreclosures and fraud. We initiated another process that raised $60 million through the Hardest Hit Fund. Then we initiated a $50 million urban revitalization initiative in Cuyahoga County that will greatly benefit Cleveland and the inner-ring suburbs. All of this money is primarily focused on the removal of vacant homes and then the re-greening of those neighborhoods.

I want to take my hat off to my friend and colleague, Jim Rokakis, whom we hired in 2011 to launch our urban program. Without Jim, very little or none of this would have happened. And, as he says, without Western Reserve none of this would have happened. Western Reserve Land Conservancy, led by Jim Rokakis and our lobbying team, has secured approximately $600 million for blight removal in Ohio since 2012. Yes, $600 million. The most recent tranche of funding, approximately $350 million, is also eligible for the abandoned apartment buildings that are littered throughout East Cleveland. Neither Jim nor Western Reserve Land Conservancy get credit for the astounding amount of funding they have brought to bear on this oft-ignored state of emergency in many of our cities. I am grateful to Jim and many others with whom he has worked so hard to highlight the plight of these neighborhoods and to actually solve the problem by removing the horrific blight. As Jim often says, you cannot build the new American city unless you get rid of the old blighted one.

Our efforts have led to the removal of more than twenty-five thousand abandoned, unlivable vacant homes, with ten thousand in Cleveland alone. You can't just take down a vacant home, leave behind a weed- and trash-infested lot, and create what we would call "blight light." It's better than blighted homes but it is still blight. What you really want to do is create a healthier place and the best way to create a healthy place is to plant trees. There was a time when Cleveland's nickname was the Forest City. Since 1940 the urban neighborhoods of the city have lost hundreds of thousands of trees, and today the city's tree canopy covers less than 20% of the land area. In 2015 the Cleveland Forest Coalition—a collaboration that includes the City of Cleveland, Cleveland Neighborhood Progress, Holden Arboretum, LAND studio, and Western Reserve Land Conservancy—developed the Cleveland Tree Plan to return Cleveland to a flourishing green city. The benefits to the people of Cleveland and the economy would be significant. Every year, even in its diminished state, the tree canopy provides amazing benefits: it captures 1.8 billion gallons of water, saves both residents and businesses $3.5 million in energy costs, eliminates 830,000 pounds of air pollution, etc. Trees improve everything. They improve the air quality, they reduce the heat island effect that literally kills urban residents in the summer, they improve public health and they revitalize neighborhoods.

People who are living in these blighted areas are living in severely distressed communities, and yet we expect them to rise above it. It is easy for a privileged white guy like me, from Shaker Heights, to say they need to pull themselves up by their bootstraps. Well, that is simply unfair; there are no bootstraps. Many kids growing up in Cleveland today don't even have access to the foundational elements of human health. So our mission is simple: we remove the bad stuff (abandoned, unlivable vacant homes) and we add more and more trees, we help communities get access to vacant land so they can create community gardens and uplifting urban farms.

Our study of biology has also informed our learning. As a society we don't often apply all the lessons of biology to humans, which is a big mistake because we are, obviously, biological organisms. We are, literally, an ecosystem of trillions of cells working in harmony with each other. When I learned that the adult human body comprised an estimated 50 trillion human cells and approximately 500 trillion non-human cells composed of a thousand different species, I was so amazed by that example of harmony. I am actually an ecosystem of a thousand species and nine out of ten of my body's cells are non-human. Then, if you extrapolate that to the human community, we are just a bunch of biological organisms cooperating to make a larger community. So to not apply the laws of biology doesn't make any sense. Two laws of biology stand out when we think about community. One is that all living things are a reflection of their environment; they are actually governed by their environment. In other words, the expression of every living thing is governed by the environment it finds itself living in. This is proven at the stem cell level where muscle cells are programed genetically to become muscle tissue, but if they are put in an environment conducive to fat cells they will become fat cells. The same thing happens with a human being: we grow to reflect the characteristics of our environment.

The second law of biology that applies to our work is that all living things naturally move away from anything they perceive as toxic, *if they can*, and move towards anything they perceive as a nutrient, if they can. It doesn't matter if it is a single cell or a human being, we are all programed to move away from that which we perceive to be toxic and towards anything we perceive to be a nutrient. That is how all life survives. When you apply that to our mission, our work becomes very simple: you have to clean up things that are perceived as bad—vacant homes, ugliness of any kind—and you have to put in things that are perceived as good such as trees, clean air, and clean water.

A friend of mine, Dave, grew up in a very distressed area in East Cleveland in the 1970s and early 1980s. He went to school in a very distressed school district. He was a gifted and hard-working athlete and got a scholarship to an all-boys private school in the 9th grade. So he came from an all-black distressed urban city environment to University School (US), which is an all-white, affluent, and privileged environment. US is a pastoral place ... peaceful, quiet, filled with trees and clean air. He came from a place filled with gun shots, screams, and scary things to a place where the teachers have time to nurture students. During his first year we were in the same class. One day he came to me for help with an algebra problem and I realized he did not know simple long division, something he should have learned in 3rd grade. So I showed him how to do it, and he immediately got it; he was very smart. He had grown up in such a tough place that no one had had time to notice that he had missed out on this fundamental math skill. That was the fall of 1983; by the fall of 1986 we were seniors and Dave was in advanced calculus, one of the best math students in the school. He was accepted by John Hopkins University. Today Dave is an emergency room doctor. What was the difference between the Dave who came to me to learn long division in the 9th grade, and the Dave who was helping me with calculus as a senior? It wasn't his genes; you can't change that. It wasn't his work ethic; he always worked hard. It wasn't his innate math mind; you either have that or you don't. The only difference was his academic environment. He still lived in distressed East Cleveland. But every single day he was in a fundamentally different academic and physical environment. Dave manifested as a different person right before our eyes. It was beautiful and inspiring.

I would have never had the insights I have about how our organization can have an impact in the communities in Cleveland if I had not met Dave. I was telling this story to a very successful African American man who grew up in the same environment as Dave, and he said, "Wow, that is the same thing that happened to me. I was a good basketball player so I went to this all-boys school called St. Joe's and I got out of that neighborhood. All of my friends from the old neighborhood, the ones who never got out, are dead or in jail." What I find so amazing is that we all try to change the individual and we try to pick off these discreet things, when all we have to do is change the fundamental environment and then everyone and everything will blossom.

Core values: what matters most

Whatever we do has to stand to reason. We do not do something just because we *think* it is right, or because it is conventional wisdom, or because that is how we've always done it; it has to stand to reason no matter what. When we problem solve, we learn first and then we come up with a hypothesis. We then test the hypothesis. If what we see does not stand to reason, then we change direction. We are brutally honest about what works. This leads to strategic insights and effective programs.

An example: if you look at the dynamics in our region, in 1950 Cuyahoga County had 1.4 million people and today we have fewer than 1.3 million; in Cleveland we had 950,000 people and today we have fewer than 400,000. Simple math tells us we have a huge problem, that people have left the city in droves. And this is despite hundreds of millions of dollars invested in various programs and efforts. These strategies are clearly not working, and yet people keep doing them. We don't do that. We make sure that our solutions stand to reason, which means, if they are not working, we modify. The biggest obstacle I have faced is that a lot of people don't want to change their mind; they want to be right even if they are wrong. In an ever-changing world, you have to be open to changing your mind. That is very hard for most people. I know it's hard for me, but I like being able to do that; it's like freedom!

Always focus on and address causes rather than effects. And when you think you are addressing causes look again because it can be very confusing. You need to get to the *root* causes. To the degree we can address causes, we know we will be exponentially more successful. That is why I believe the work we do is so essential to communities. There are a lot of people doing a great job addressing the effects, and they are providing a great service to individuals. But our strength and our role is to identify and address the causes. Urban reforestation is a great example of that in action. A lot of the human distress that we see in poor neighborhoods in our cities is because there are no trees in those neighborhoods. As a society most of us are raised to focus on effects rather than the root causes. So how do you help people to understand that the lack of trees contributes to the human distress in their communities? We try to help communities understand the cause and effect dynamic of environmentally distressed communities. We rely on research. There are thousands of new studies that prove the detrimental effects of an inadequate tree canopy. They are not part of the conventional wisdom yet but soon they will be. Soon people will understand that sometimes you need to plant trees to save a school district.

Brutal honesty. We constantly challenge ourselves to be honest with each other, with the community and with ourselves. Without being disrespectful, we need to tell people things that are not conventional or popular at the time. The vacant home situation is a great example; people don't like talking about the problem of vacant, abandoned homes. They don't like talking about demolishing vacant homes and yet we have thousands of them littering these neighborhoods. There is a great anecdote we had from the St. Luke's neighborhood: we were in the community interviewing the kids and asked them, "If you had a million dollars to improve the neighborhood what would you do?" They said, "The first thing we would do is get rid of the 'bandos'; all these abandoned homes are killing us. They are scary, that's where the bad guys hang out, that's where the bad stuff happens." Children know that we need to get rid of the vacant homes. But some decision-makers have an aversion to it. It sends out a negative message: it means the city is losing population; it means we might take down historic homes. And yet the brutal truth is that if we don't take those homes down we will never move the needle in the right direction.

Everybody is equal and everybody has strengths that complement other people. Nobody is smarter or better than anyone else. We just have to figure out how a person's strength can be celebrated and how a weakness can be avoided. For my part, I'm "administratively challenged" so we don't want me focused on a lot of administrative stuff. We have a fundamental belief that everyone is trying to do the right thing, yet we all have different inclinations and strengths. The culture we have been raised with—that everything is about individual effort and individual talent—is actually a myth. Everybody is equal, everything is connected, and everyone is dependent on everyone else at some level.

Everything is about people, meaning what we do is done through people and everything we do is for people. This could be confusing because you could say that our work is about preserving biodiversity, not about people. But without people we wouldn't have to bother preserving biodiversity or saving a rare species of bird. Without people, the birds would be just fine. Our work is really about people; our mission is about creating harmony between a lot of people and a healthy environment, each supporting and nurturing the other. We have 4 million people in our service area, so figuring out how to realize harmony between people and the environment is challenging. We seek harmony, not balance, because balance to me is a zero sum game. Harmony, however, implies an ever-improving and complementary state of health, of wholeness.

Defining moments

As a child I loved being in the woods. My dad and I would backpack in the wilderness a lot and when I wasn't backpacking, I was playing in the woods somewhere. I was always drawn to the outdoors. In high school, I was drawn to biology and I worked with a professor on brook trout studies, planting trees, and making maple syrup. It was called the natural areas program. My family lived in Cleveland Heights but I went to school in the countryside. Then I went to college in Vermont and I was inspired by the beauty of that state.

After college I didn't know what I wanted to do so I backpacked for a year with a friend around the western United States, western Canada, and Alaska. During that trip I read a lot and thought a lot. I remember one day I was walking in a national park and crossed over into a national forest which was adjacent to it. The national park was in a pristine natural state, and I felt so peaceful and whole. All of a sudden we crossed into a national forest that looked as if it had just been bombed with napalm. It was shocking, I had a visceral reaction to all of the destruction, thousands and thousands of acres of trees cut away. It was awful. I remember thinking at that moment, I am going to help to preserve land. I was reading a book at the time by Barry Lopez called *The Rediscovery of North America*[1] where he said, don't just get angry, think about what you are angry about and figure out how to address it. Do something about it. So I ended up writing a personal statement of purpose about preserving land to help people heal and grow. I was 22 when I wrote my statement of purpose (see the end of this chapter). As I tell all my interns, be careful what you write down, because it's going to happen.

After that I returned to Vermont where my girlfriend (now wife) was in medical school. I had a meeting with the president of the Vermont Land Trust. I asked him, "If you were me and you wanted to become

1   Lopez, B. (1990). *The Rediscovery of North America*. New York: Vintage.

you, what would you do now, at my age?" Without any hesitation he said, "I'd become a fundraiser, because that's the salve that cures all ill." So I became a fundraiser at the University of Vermont, and then at Case Western Reserve University Law School. Everything evolved from that day I was backpacking out west and came upon that devastated forest. That was the catalyst for writing my statement of purpose. That set me on my journey to understanding that the environment governs our expression as people, that it governs who we become and how we evolve. That may have been on an intuitive level the reason I was so passionate about the environment, but I did not consciously put the pieces together until much later. At that time, I did not understand that environmental equality is essential to human equality.

Biggest obstacle

As a nonprofit it is hard to attract the resources we require to provide the services that our communities need so we rely on philanthropy, which is limited. We need to figure out how to unleash more market capital, as opposed to charitable support, to fund our mission and programs. To the degree that we can do that, we can maximize the amount of work we can get done. Half of our budget comes from market-driven revenues. That is progress, and yet we could do so much more.

Greatest lessons learned

First, **never lose your temper**. When we lose our temper we are naturally in a fight or flight response. Unless we are in a life-threatening situation, we are at our worst when we are in this response. Biologically speaking, our prefrontal cortex shuts down and automatically all of our blood is sent to the rear-brain, which is our aggressive brain area. The fight or flight response debilitates our ability to think clearly, to be strategic, to learn. We become animals. Yes, it feels good—we have adrenaline rushing through us and we feel powerful and smart, but we are intellectually incapacitated when we lose our temper. All of my mistakes have been made when I lose my temper. Fight or flight also debilitates our immune and our digestive systems. If you talk with people who live in an environment in which a fight or flight response is a way of life, they often talk of stomach problems and chronic illness. The immune system and digestive system are both very energy intensive and completely shut down when you are in a fight or flight mode so you have the energy to fight or escape the danger.

Imagine you are a 12-year-old boy living in a bad neighborhood on the east side of Cleveland. You are surrounded by scary things and there is very little beauty or peace in your environment. You are constantly in a fight or flight response and you wind up with a messed up digestive system and a very aggressive and reactive pattern of behavior. Your blood is preferentially sent to your hindbrain, which is the seat of reflex and aggression. Your prefrontal cortex—which is the seat of reason, learning, and creativity—is chronically deprived of blood and nutrients. You are constantly immune suppressed so you are susceptible to colds and cancers. It is nearly impossible for a 12-year-old boy to thrive in an environment that activates the fight or flight response.

By allowing people to live in these stress-filled environments, we are creating this biological assault that people are not aware of. If this 12-year-old boy goes to the doctor complaining of stomach problems, the doctor examines his stomach and other parts of his body. The truth is that the doctor needs to examine his environment; that is the cause of the distress, not the stomach. The doctor needs to ask him, "What is your home like? Are you getting beat up at school?" But the doctor just looks at his stomach, and the stomach has nothing to do with why he has digestive problems. His stomach aches are the manifestation of constant stress.

Bottom-line, when you allow yourself to lose your temper, you are debilitating your intellect, your digestive system and your immune system. The 12-year-old boy in the distressed environment does not have a choice. For him, survival requires a fight or flight response. But for many of us, it is an option. It is better to choose not to lose your temper.

Second, **karma exists**. Karma is the law of cause and effect; everything you put out in the world is a cause that will lead to a responsive effect. You should never put bad out because you are likely to get bad back either directly or indirectly. Always be as good, as honest, and as virtuous as possible. Not only is it going to make your life easier, it

> will make the world a little bit better. We need to be very mindful of the power of karma. I believe it is a natural law; what you give is what you get, and what you become.

What I learned from Rich Cochran

I walk away from this entire experience with a big "ah ha!" I have always believed that what is on the inside of a person comes out on the outside. But I now understand that what is on the outside, literally the physical environment, critically impacts what is on the inside of a person. This makes for a vicious cycle that whole cultures are caught in with little opportunity to break out of their own accord. This cycle must be understood and it must be broken. Western Reserve Land Conservancy, in partnership with the city and community partners, is taking courageous steps to reverse this malady that plagues so many of our urban cities, and for that I am deeply grateful.

Rich wrote his mission and vision for his life following a crucial defining moment in the national park. He later used his statement to gain entrance into a master's program. I found Rich's Statement of Purpose to be compelling, inspiring, and instructive as well as foretelling. His mission and vision, almost to a word, became his reality. I want to close this chapter by sharing some excerpts from Rich's Statement of Purpose. Rich wrote this when he was 22 years old.

Rich's Statement of Purpose

The earth is our home, where we live, and we must view it as such in our study of ecology as well as in our daily lives. The distinction between home and house is for me the key to learning how to live well, in and on our earth; it is a value distinction, one which draws on how one would treat his own home as opposed to how he would treat a random house standing on a street corner. I suggest that one would treat his own home with respect, with long term viability in mind, and one would approach the random house with indifference.

With the above distinction in mind, I would like to introduce to you my long range vision for myself. I want to found (as in create), develop and lead a foundation devoted to preserving and conserving our scarce natural resources while developing and facilitating programs that enhance our unlimited human resources. My ideal foundation, a non-politically aligned organization, would purchase and conserve wild lands and then develop on and around those lands "place-specific" programming within the fields of leadership development, self-development, environmental education.

The vision above, which has become my personal mission, came to me in a very rough form during early 1992 and crystalized during the last six to nine months. In 1991 and 1992, I backpacked and mountain biked all over North America with a companion. During our travels we encountered the most pristine wilderness areas in North America and the most abused ecosystems in the world. One week we slept in forests and mountains that stretched unbroken for miles, and the next we stood in a clear cut area that could be seen from the moon! Northwestern rivers, once crystal clear ran thick with mud and run-off. We walked along the boundary line of a National Park and a National Forest in Washington where the Forest side was clear cut right up to the ancient trees protected by the Park Land designation. The contrast left us gasping, and angry. Instead of directing that anger at people, though, I decided then and there that I would redirect my anger and make it a positive energy that would work to prevent atrocities as above, committed by men against nature purely for wealth-building, from happening again.

It is said that knowledge bears a price. In my case, the knowledge of what we have done and continue to do to our earth has shattered what was once a blissful acceptance of the status quo. During my first three years of college I planned unquestioningly to go into a traditional white collar career such as big business, perhaps law or maybe banking. Virtually everyone I knew did that. So why should I do anything different? I didn't even know that there was anything else. Well, I have been disillusioned of late, and for that I am grateful.

What I want to do now is gain more knowledge of our natural resources, of our environment—what it is scientifically and biologically, where we stand ecologically and where we are going if we stay on our present course. I want to understand the hard sciences. I want to be able to talk with scientists about soil horizons, thermodynamics, biological oxygen demand and photosynthesis. I want to talk with ecologists about population dynamics, mutualisms and optimal foraging. I want to advance a dialogue about enhancing biodiversity through holistic ecosystem management, and I want to understand the advantages and limitations of landscape corridors with respect to species preservation and habitat maintenance. Then and only then, will I feel capable of achieving my ultimate mission, that of a conservation/education foundation head, as a steward or our natural resources.

Junior Enterprise World Movement: 45,000 passionate social
entrepreneurs

11
Junior Enterprise World Movement: millennials leading

The Junior Enterprise (JE) movement was founded in Paris, France, in 1967. It has grown into a thriving global network of 40,000 passionate student members, in 840 enterprises, spread across 40 countries including Brazil, France, Germany, Belgium, Poland, Romania, Netherlands, Sweden, Austria, Italy, Portugal, Switzerland, UK, Croatia, Tunisia, Denmark, Spain, Canada, Mexico, and China, and in 2015 the first US chapters were formed. Junior Enterprises are nonpolitical, nonprofit enterprises that serve their members by providing them with opportunities to develop entrepreneurial and business skills while they are still in university. They do this by running small and medium-sized businesses that provide services such as engineering and marketing to their local companies, institutions, and communities. They are entirely student-led, student-managed, and student-funded, and each enterprise is affiliated with a university or business school. They have formal structures, organizational systems, and processes locally, regionally, and country by country, similar to most global businesses.

They have two guiding umbrella organizations that come together to form the global network. The European Confederation of Junior Enterprises (JADE) includes 20,000 social entrepreneurs from 280 student-run small- to medium-sized enterprises (SMEs) across 14 European countries. They also serve as a catalyst to help incubate and develop Junior Enterprises around the world. Brasil Júnior is

FIGURE 11.1   Junior Enterprise World Day: every year on November 22, the Junior Enterprises World Network comes together through social media to celebrate the Junior Enterprise concept

the world's largest confederation of Junior Enterprises with over 15,000 social entrepreneurs from 245 Junior Enterprises throughout Brazil, working together to help co-create a thriving Brazil.

This global network of 45,000 young millennial social entrepreneurs is very special. They are bonded by a compelling shared vision and shared values and they share a strong sense of identity and pride in the Junior Enterprise worldwide movement. They have become a passionate, powerful force for change, or what I call DreamMakers.

I was first exposed to the Junior Enterprise World Movement when Ryo Penna, then the President of Brasil Júnior, invited me to give the keynote speech at the closing plenary at the Junior Enterprise World Conference in 2012 held in Paraty, Brazil, and hosted by Brasil Júnior. Over 2,000 Junior Entrepreneurs from around the world gathered in that beautiful, charming village to explore their theme "One World, One Network" with a tagline "Evolve, Undertake, Transform." It was that visionary theme that led me to say "yes" to the invitation to fly over 5,000 miles, get in the car with a total stranger who drove me four hours through jungle and mountains, to spend five days with a large group of twenty-somethings that I had never heard of before. Thank God I did! As soon as I stepped out of the car I was engulfed in a whirlwind of powerful, positive energy, and for the next three days I was introduced to an incredible, optimistic group of millennial social entrepreneurs committed to changing their communities and the world. I came home feeling hopeful and grateful and a huge fan of these amazing young leaders.

In July 2016, I had the privilege of giving the opening and closing address at their Junior Enterprise World Conference held in Florianópolis, Brazil. Their theme was Lead the Co-Era, Lead the Cooperation. Over 3,500 passionate, optimistic millennial entrepreneurs from 20 countries came together for four days (Fig. 11.2). Their purpose was to envision together ways in which they could make a positive impact on the world. This was no average conference. It was highly collaborative, filled with experiential learning and public service opportunities, and there were lots of celebrations.

FIGURE 11.2   Junior Enterprise World Conference, 2016

To say I was impressed is a huge understatement. It was hosted by the Federação das Empresas Juniores do Estado de Santa Catarina (Federation of Junior Enterprises of Santa Catarina State). Led by their president Yuri Kuzniecow, these highly competent, creative, and committed young entrepreneurs planned, managed, staffed, and secured the funding for this amazing event, and they were all volunteers. I can say unequivocally: this was the best conference I have ever attended.

Over the years I have continued to communicate with and support the Junior Enterprise World Movement. I have grown to love and respect these amazing young entrepreneurs. I have stayed connected to them because they feed my soul and lift my spirit. I have much to learn from them and when they seek my counsel I give my time and advice freely with a grateful heart.

It is my pleasure to share the voices of a few of these very special Junior Entrepreneurs, DreamMakers, charting the future of this brand new and better world. Meet four leaders of the Junior Enterprise Movement: Ryoichi Oka Penna, Pedro Henrique Lima do Nascimento, Camille Delesalle, and Mehdi Ben Miloud.

 ## Meet Ryoichi Oka Penna, advisory board member and former President, Brasil Júnior

Ryo's vision for the Junior Enterprise (JE) network

I'd like to do the math to put my vision in perspective. Currently there are roughly 7.3 million undergraduate students in Brazil and 15,000 are Junior Entrepreneurs; this means that the JE population in Brazil is only 0.02% of the total undergraduate population. My biggest dream is to make Brasil Júnior more relevant and involve more people in the movement because I strongly believe in the Brasil Júnior model and I have seen how it benefits people and our society. It's not only the question of the number of people; it's about broadening the depth and breadth of service that we provide. The main job of JE is to

FIGURE 11.3   Ryo Penna, advisory board member and former President, Brasil Júnior

deliver consulting services to SMEs, which make up 99% of the firms in Brazil. My dream is that our services will help these SMEs leverage their results, generate more employment, generate more income for families, especially families living in poverty, and do all this in an ethical, sustainable manner that benefits businesses, people, the environment, and our country. My highest aspiration is for JE to be seen, valued, and recognized as a powerful change catalyst for Brazilian society and the economy. I have a vision in which we develop people that have the capacity, skills, values, and character to go out into the world and positively impact Brazil in every facet of our society. I dream that someday we will have a president of Brazil who came through JE; that most of the CEOs come from JEs; and that the actions that positively change and impact Brazil come from the hearts and minds of former Brasil Júnior entrepreneurs. I want this because I so deeply believe in the Brasil Júnior values. Brazil has a lot of poor people and few rich people. We don't want the rich people to be poorer, but we want the poor people to be richer.

All people should have their basic needs met: health, education, and security.

The Brasil Júnior network can impact society on three levels. First, the network of Junior Entrepreneurs can foster entrepreneurship within their universities. Second, we can provide consulting services to SMEs. And third, JE can become engaged in social causes. We have a former Junior Entrepreneur who created a program to hire the best talent in Brazil to work in the public sector. Her dream is to have not only great CEOs and executives but also great governors, mayors, and other public policymakers. Brasil Júnior has an overarching shared mission to be the main university movement in Brazil that develops the best leaders in the country so that each enterprise has a lot of autonomy over how they fulfill the mission.

Core values

The values that matter to me most are: **humility** because it allows me to be open to learning; **gratefulness**: I learned to always be grateful and open-hearted; and **conviction**, which for me means being open and asking a lot of questions but being confident about a few things. For example, I believe that this generation in Brazil can *be* the change and *do* the change we need in this country. This is a movement that implies that we are not a generation that is standing still.

Defining moments

When I first joined JE in 2010, I heard them talk about a Junior Enterprise World Conference (JEWC) that was taking place in Milan, Italy, and I knew I had to be there. I was 19 years old and I had never even been on a plane but I started to work to translate our workshops into English so we could share them at the conference, and I started looking for a sponsor to fund my trip. I knocked on everyone's door and finally one of the mangers at the university agreed to pay my airfare. When I arrived in Italy I realized I was in the right place at the right time; it was one of the happiest days of my life. The conference was an amazing experience.

We were invited to make a one-hour presentation about how Brasil Júnior was fostering entrepreneurship and shaping entrepreneurial leaders for the future. The presentation ended up lasting four hours because they were so amazed at the work we were doing that they canceled all the other presenters. They were especially interested and impressed that we had passed a bill in the national senate that had set forth a legal status for Brasil Júnior. It was a long process; I had to negotiate with 40 senators and it was very difficult but we were successful. It is now called the Junior Enterprise Law. The national government formally recognizes and supports the creation of JEs, which enables public universities to foster and support them. We were very proud of this accomplishment.

The next defining moment happened when I learned that the 2012 JEWC was going to be in Brazil and I decided I wanted to be a part of the team that planned the conference. I ended up becoming chair of the planning team and it was an awesome experience. That led to my decision to run for and win the presidency of the Federation of Junior Enterprises of Minas Gerais, usually known as FEJEMG, which is the biggest federation of Brazil. The main reason for that decision was that, after the amazing experience I had while organizing the 2012 conference, I realized I could impact more people with a clear vision to keep on empowering and catalyzing the rise of new DreamMakers. In 2015 I cofounded ReOrg with Pedro Nascimento, the former President of Junior Enterprise of Rio de Janeiro and Vice President of Brasil Júnior; I'm sure we are going to co-create a lot of new and exciting defining moments.

Greatest obstacles

The greatest obstacle has been that the public universities have considered us a private organization so JE has not been well understood and thus not well supported here in Brazil. Hopefully the new law will help to rectify this situation.

Another obstacle is that JEs primarily have people from higher economic communities. Most people in JEs are from households that have money so they don't have to work while attending university; they can invest some of their time in JE. We don't get paid so if their parents don't have money, most students have to work while they go to school, meaning that they don't have the time or the resources to work in a JE. This is a big challenge that we need to find a way to overcome.

Greatest lessons learned

First, when you have open-minded people who are hungry for knowledge and new experiences, the sky is the limit. It is amazing to be a part of a high-energy team; you feel you can accomplish anything. Second, you don't have to have a lot of experience to do a good job if you are open to learning. Third, I got to know young people from countries in North America and across Europe and I realized that Brazilians are so uncomfortable with the status quo and all the problems we have that we have a higher level of energy and engagement with social causes than most other Junior Entrepreneurs.

The last thing I want to say is that I owe most of who I am and what I know to the Junior Enterprise movement. Before joining JE, I knew very little. The experiences JE gave me have been awesome, from my first plane ride, to presenting in Geneva, to lobbying senators in the national government, to dealing with CEOs. This experience gave me, and my colleague Pedro Nascimento, the confidence to create our consulting firm, ReOrg. We collaborate with leaders on the sustainability of organizations through the discovery and development of values and cultures This has been an amazing journey and I am deeply grateful.

Meet Pedro Henrique Lima do Nascimento, advisory board member and former Vice President, Brasil Júnior

Pedro's vision and highest aspiration

As a 24-year-old, I have not yet come up with the words that define my purpose, but I know what I aspire to become. First, I want to serve a cause greater than myself. That is why I love working with organizations and everyone associated with them to flourish: employees, leaders, customers, suppliers, etc. Working to help create environments that enable people to be the best version of themselves—that is what really

FIGURE 11.4   Pedro Henrique Lima do Nascimento, advisory board member and former Vice President, Brasil Júnior

motivates me. I think organizations, in their pure form, are the greatest invention of mankind. They are a way for people to work together with shared vision, values, and goals, to enable them to do something that matters to them and at the same time become the best version of themselves. Somehow we lost our way; we need to return to the true purpose of organizations. My goal is to help us to reclaim that purpose.

My dream for Brasil Júnior is to develop leaders that can lead every sector of society in Brazil. Let me share a quick story as to why I have this vision. I almost did not become VP of Brasil Júnior in 2013. I felt at the time that I had accomplished great results and that was enough, it was time to leave. I also felt that Ryo Pena was the best person for the presidency. Ryo then talked to me and convinced me that the VP was responsible for developing the people management and organizational development processes and systems that enable people to flourish within an organization to develop a strong culture. I lit up. I realized that this could be what I was looking for next. When I was elected VP, my vision was "How can I make Brasil Júnior the most admired organization in the JE movement in the world—who we are and how we work?"

We developed the Brasil Júnior Way: the Brasil Júnior Way of Being, the Brasil Júnior Way of Thinking and the Brasil Júnior Way of Doing. I began to notice that people started organically adopting it. It acted like a fractal and started popping up all over the place. I started to understand my contribution was helping people live by sharing vision and values. Then I realized that we had a responsibility to not just develop leaders for Brasil Júnior, we had a responsibility to develop leaders for the country of Brazil. I looked around and saw some excellent young leaders in Brasil Júnior that I truly want to see become president of my country someday.

My dream for Brasil Júnior is to develop leaders that can lead every sector of society in Brazil; we need the next entrepreneurial leader to create the next Facebook, to lead the best NGOs. Imagine a president of Brazil that is not there for the power but rather because he or she is passionate about making a difference in people's lives. Imagine leaders of big companies that are there because they want to make a difference in people's lives and for the planet. Of course they will make money, but they are there to make a difference.

The legacy Brasil Júnior can leave for Brazil is the development of leaders who lead with meaning and passion. We are beginning to see this dream come true because we have Brasil Júnior alumni leading organizations in every sector of our society. We have the power in our hands to bridge this leadership gap in the 21st century.

Defining moments

I was born in a small city in Brazil. I lived a normal life, I got good grades but I didn't have anything that motivated me. I had planned to go college and follow the status quo: get my degree, become an engineer, work in a huge company, and one day become a director and live my life spending money. Just before I went to college my brother was diagnosed with leukemia and that caused me to reflect on my own life. I started to question if my life had any meaning and I decided I needed to find something meaningful to devote my life to. In the first week of college I was introduced to JE and during that orientation, I decided it was something worth putting my time, my effort, and my dreams into. I saw this 20-year-old from JE give an awesome presentation to the group and my eyes lit up. He was very professional, articulate, and confident; I decided then and there, I wanted to be that kind of person, I wanted to be able to engage people like that. My main goal was to develop myself and learn to do what he did.

My vision evolved when I got my first leadership position. I had the audacity at 20 to be elected president of my JE of 60 people. That experience gave me a purpose. When I took the position, the enterprise had been stagnant and I knew it was important for us to grow. JEs are non-profits so it wasn't about the money, rather we needed big challenges. Overcoming the challenges would make us better leaders and prepare us to do great things in the world. That's when I got very passionate about leadership and management because to create the conditions for ordinary people to do extraordinary things was the way for me to contribute to the world. I wanted to create a great system to develop great people and that would be my sustainable contribution to the world.

When I first started the job I realized we did not have anything to glue us together. Everyone was working hard and contributing but we did not have a shared vision and our values were stuck on the wall; we were not living them. I felt we were hypocritical. At our first general meeting I gathered all our results, our indicators and compared them to other JEs and we all realized we were not as good as we thought we were. We needed to take off our rose-colored glasses. People thought we were the best because we were the best engineering school in Brazil. It was very risky and some people hated me after that but as Peter Senge, the thought leader on whole systems thinking would say, we needed to understand our current reality. Next, in an appreciative way, we redefined our values to clarify what we stood for. We developed values that really represented who we were instead of values such as "excellence" and "transparency." We decided on "We are thirsty for knowledge" and "Everyone should be known by anyone."

We developed the processes and the systems that engendered the behavior we wanted and that would sustain our culture. For example, in our selection process, it was more important that people lived our values than had technical skills. The main processes were: select the best people who live our values; define clear, big goals that would stretch us; engage people in discovering the possibilities; and figure out what was working and what was not working, and together decide what we needed to do to improve. I also started to develop myself—this is one thing that defines me. I got lots of mentors to help me and I read a lot of books. As Harry Truman said "Not all readers are leaders, but all leaders are readers." Before I became president I was talking with a good friend of mine, Marcus Barão, and it was one of those life-changing talks. We were talking about our dreams and goals and I told him I wanted to become president of the enterprise and he asked me, "Pedro how many books have you read in the last year?" I told him I had read one. He told me something I will never forget: "Do you really want to be a leader that does not study and prepare himself?" That struck a chord in me. I realized that I could have the biggest dreams for myself and the enterprise but if I didn't develop myself, it would all be for nothing. I would only be a motivated guy that couldn't do anything. Over the next year I read 36 books and lots of articles. Our results the following first year was amazing. Our revenue grew 260% and we completed 70% more projects. We won first place for the best managed organization in the Rio Federation; we also won first prize for the strongest culture nationwide. What makes me proudest is that the enterprise has sustained that growth and its strong culture.

A big defining moment for me was being a part of the planning team for the Junior Enterprise World Conference in Paraty in 2012. A week after I became president of my enterprise, Marcus Barão came to me and asked me to join the planning team. It was a massive mission. We needed to bring 2,000 Junior Entrepreneurs from all over the world to a remote village, four hours from Rio de Janeiro. We needed to raise a ridiculous amount of money, half a million reals (about US$240,000), in one year. We had to coordinate the accommodation for 2,000 people with 20 inns and 30 restaurants. We needed to construct a conference site because the village did not have any place large enough to accommodate us. It was crazy. I said yes to Barão because when he talked about this seemingly impossible dream you could feel his energy and his eyes were sparkling. I knew I had to do it. A couple of days before the conference, as we walked to the conference structure, I remember crossing the street and I looked up and saw that huge, beautiful, shining, white structure. We jumped up and down, hugged each other and I said, "Dude, how did we do this?" It was a life-changing moment; any notion we had of not being able to accomplish something great, with a team of like-minded people just dissipated. Ever since then I have believed we can do anything!

Greatest obstacles

One year ago I would have said being young was the greatest obstacle, being taken seriously when consulting CEOs and their organizations at 25 years old. But in 2015 Ryo Penna and I founded a consulting company and that is exactly what we are doing.

Greatest lesson learned

You can make the impossible dream a reality.

Meet Camille Delesalle, advisory board member and former President of the National Confederation of Junior Enterprises for France

Camille's vision and highest aspiration

Let me share a little history or context. The Junior Enterprise movement is more than 46 years old. The first Confederation of Junior Enterprises was held in 1969 by a French business school. The mission was and is "To help students find and discover the working world to professionalize students." Back then internships did not exist in France, so the Junior

FIGURE 11.5
Camille Delesalle,
Former President
of the National
Confederation of
Junior Enterprises
for France

Enterprise movement was the only way for students to be exposed to the world of business before they entered the professional world of work.

Today we are much more than just an avenue to gain professional experience before graduating from university. Today we are a movement. Everyone I talk to in Junior Enterprise gets very animated and passionate about the movement, which represents wholeness. To have a movement we need to all move together in one direction. It's a huge movement of people, ideas and ideals. We are young and fast-moving so everything is dynamic. We are really energetic. When you talk to a Junior Entrepreneur the main thing you will see and feel is "passion." It's like an ocean, when you get in the flow, you get swept up in it and you can't get out of it; in fact you don't want to get out of it because it is a great feeling to be a part of a movement that is trying to change the world.

Our vision is that we will be in every school in the world and every student, regardless of their social or economic status will have the opportunity to be a part of the JE movement. Today JE is elitist and only a few can gain access to it. I would like the movement to become more inclusive so it can benefit more people. It makes me very sad when my friends feel regret that they were not a part of JE. I have learned so much about myself, about people, and about how to work in teams. This is a unique experience and it needs to be available to far more young people around the world.

In my vision, the JE movement will become the voice of students around the world! When anyone thinks about youth, about entrepreneurship, about students, about evolution, they would think about JEs and they would seek the input of Junior Entrepreneurs on issues and opportunities that face our world. We are students that care about the world. We have a lot to offer. Our perspective on the world today and what it could be in the future is very valuable. We are volunteers; no individual gets paid in JE, and the money we make goes into the enterprise so basically we are managing volunteers. That is a real challenge, but you learn a great deal from managing volunteers because you have to create an environment that engages everyone and engenders passion. We are not getting paid so the work becomes about the difference we make to people's businesses and to their lives. It's about the people we have the privilege to work with, how you treat them, and how you make them feel. This is what we get in exchange for volunteering our skills, energy, and time and it's tremendously meaningful. In my vision the way we work would change the definition of leadership everywhere.

Core values

Fraternity is important to me. We need each other; I truly need people around to help me and I need to be able to help people. That interaction is where real satisfaction and a sense of community is derived. We need that sense of fraternity and community because the best ideas come out of collaborative conversations and the best results come from collaborative actions. I try to lead this way; sometimes this approach is harder, but it is always more effective.

Identity is important to me. Twice a year we hold a national congress that unites 1,000 JEs. Every year the confederation chooses three main values to work on and one of our values this year is Identity. We will work to make sure every single Junior Entrepreneur truly feels they are a part of this huge movement, and that we are a huge family. We want all Junior Enterprises to feel connected and to help each other.

Humility is also one of my core values. With everything I am doing, I feel that nothing is going to stop me, but I am also paying attention to maintaining my humility. I am only 21 years old and I have a lot of responsibility and a lot of power. I am meeting incredible people; we are doing amazing things. But it is important for me to be "me" and to be modest.

I also value **working together for the greater good**. One example is that our enterprise helped a man who wanted a windmill in his backyard to create his own energy, so we helped him to design and build it. We helped make his dream come true. That is a wonderful feeling.

Defining moments

When I was preparing for college I wanted to be a veterinarian. I love animals and I love taking care of things so this seemed like the right fit for me. I wanted to specialize in taking care of horses but when I saw how humans treated horses I was appalled. To see them abuse horses to train them or make them run fast was heartbreaking. I knew that I could never be at ease around people who treated animals like that. I decided not to become a vet because of the people, not the horses. I could not feel a sense of fraternity with people who hurt animals.

Then at the very last moment I decided to become an engineer. When I first got to engineering school I thought I had made a big mistake. The work included a lot of mechanics and physics. The school is called Arts et Métiers, we are called *"gadz'arts,"* meaning guys from the arts. I felt I did not fit in but after one week I was in love with the school. We were taught the value of fraternity; we had to learn everyone's name and where they came from, and we truly learned to work together. I learned a great deal about myself and about other people. The experience was so powerful. I felt that nothing could stop me, I was invincible. It was not the engineering that got me excited; it was learning to work with people. That's why I joined JE, to learn more about leadership, teamwork and relationships. Six months after I joined JE I was elected president of my enterprise and this gave me the opportunity to learn how to lead people.

I loved it, I was inspired to get up in the morning and work all day, and sometimes all night on projects. I found it so fascinating.

Then I met the president of the French Confederation, Confédération Nationale des Junior-Entreprises, who talked so passionately about his work. Today I am president of the confederation. The confederation includes all the Junior Enterprises of France: we have 117 JEs across France and over 20,000 members. We are the largest student movement in France and we are the largest confederation in the world apart from Brazil—they are exploding!

I am not sure what I will do after this experience. It is hard because I have learned so much at JE. I am not drawn to working for a huge company, I think I want to start my own small firm that helps people to connect and nurture their relationships. I want to be able to contribute to something meaningful with my work and have a quality life so I am leaning towards my own small firm where I can do both.

Greatest lessons learned

Nothing is impossible. I used to think that if you work hard you will get what you deserve, but now I know that you don't always; if you work hard you will get what you want or need, but only if you ask for it. Now I am not afraid to ask for what I want. Junior Enterprise has become my life and I have learned lot through this experience. I have become more confident about a lot of things so I am not stressed any more. Now if I have a problem I focus on the solution and move on to the next problem. This is something that I am doing in other areas of my life now, with my friends, with my family, and it has really changed my life. Not panicking but instead focusing on a solution. This entire journey is about more than Junior Enterprise—it is my life.

Meet Mehdi Ben Miloud, advisory board member and former President, Junior Enterprises of Tunisia (JET)

JUNIOR ENTERPRISES OF TUNISIA

Mehdi's vision and highest aspiration

Junior Enterprises of Tunisia (JET) officially became part of the JE movement in April 2012. We are the first and the only confederation in Africa. Our mission is to coordinate the Junior Enterprise movement in Tunisia, give it the necessary support to help it to work efficiently and to grow the network. We have 25 JEs and 1,000 members. My vision is to build enough JE Federations in Africa to have an African Confederation in five years.

I joined the movement in September 2011 in the JE in my university, Checotah Business School, which was the first business school in Tunisia. In March 2012, a Tunisian Confederation of Junior Enterprises was created. The acronym, JET, is an amusing metaphor for how fast the

FIGURE 11.6   Mehdi Ben Miloud, Former President of Junior Enterprises of Tunisia

movement is growing there; already there are 17 initiatives, of which six are certified Junior Enterprises. This impressive growth is mostly due to the amazing enthusiasm for the JE concept that one can observe there. In JET's first national meeting, at a time when the country only counted six initiatives, 300 Junior Entrepreneurs gathered to think, exchange, and collaborate. In their second meeting, despite it being held in an exams period, 250 students gladly celebrated the JE movement in the city of Hammamet. JET has received support from the Tunisian government to carry out its activities. In order to audit the Tunisian JEs and ensure high quality standards we have partnered with a Tunisian audit company and are now looking for new partners. Making sure that entrepreneurship develops well in Tunisia is one of the priorities of the European Commission. As stated by the European Commission, the fast-paced development of the Junior Enterprise movement in this country is of utmost importance and JADE is therefore investing all necessary resources to contribute to this development.

My dream is to have an African Federation for the entire continent. On the road to accomplishing this ultimate dream, our goal is to gain support from the government for JET, here in Tunisia. Since the revolution it has been hard to establish a sustainable government in Tunisia and thus a sustainable relationship with JET has not been possible. The main focus right now is to gain that government's support. That will enable us to enlarge our representation and do big things such as create jobs, improve social conditions, and generate economic development. The poverty in Africa is terrible; we could make a small dent in this massive social problem.

In my vision I imagine the African Federation of Junior Enterprise influencing the youth of Africa to think from a social standpoint. We will develop social entrepreneurship and have sponsorship from the government and businesses; we will gain the credibility of businesses around the world. This could be a self-rising movement. I am really impressed with the Brazilian JE movement which has worked very hard and successfully gained its government's support. From an economic and social standpoint, we are similar to Brazil. My vision is that we duplicate its model.

Defining moments

In high school, I was a sports guy; I was really looking to get a basketball scholarship, go to the United States and, if I was lucky, join the National Basketball Association. Sports were my passion. Then in 2011, I severely injured my knee and my basketball dream was over. I desperately needed something to replace basketball. I was walking home from school and there was a Junior Enterprise stand and the Junior Entrepreneurs started to explain the movement. I joined the movement while still on crutches. They used to call me Captain Mehdi. The JE movement totally changed my life. My vision for my future completely shifted. I have transformed from a guy who was lost, because of a shattered basketball dream, to a guy who is really passionate about a mission that can change our country and can change the world. I believe that the JE movement has the capacity to reach 7 billion people. If we can make a difference in Africa, this movement can catalyze visions and impact societies around the world—the sky is the limit. Imagine the JE movement as a global social and economic ecosystem. This is my vision for the JE movement.

Core values

The core values that I hold dear are **leadership**, **entrepreneurship**, and **reaching people**. These values catalyze community building to positively impact people's lives.

Lessons learned

The major lesson I have learned is that the Junior Enterprise movement, not basketball, means the world to me; it has been life changing.

What I learned from Junior Entrepreneurs

The Junior Enterprise movement, is a way of life, a community of people who share a common global vision and shared values and are using their entrepreneurial skills and spirit to co-create a flourishing future. For a moment the JE movement took me back to my college days. Being a baby boomer, I reflected on the days when we banded together in protest at the injustices in our world including the war in Vietnam and racial and sex discrimination. But I realized something is very different about these remarkable young people. They are not protesting: together they are co-creating the future: entrepreneurship, collaboration, and innovation are their "weapons." Most importantly, they are smarter, faster, far more informed, more connected, more hopeful, and more courageous than any former generation in the history of the world. They understand on a very deep level that we are all connected and they are committed to putting their vision for the world, their values, and the momentum of the Junior Enterprise worldwide movement to work to co-create a world where people and the planet have the opportunity to flourish

We have been culturally conditioned to believe that young people must wait their turn to lead. That would be a very long wait, given the tenacious hold many current leaders in our world have on the past. Isn't it time to challenge this assumption? The world has dramatically and fundamentally changed and as a friend of mine put it, "the past has relinquished its hold on the future." We need younger leaders to stand with us as peers on this journey, with their fresh eyes and clean hearts. They are the "end point of evolution" and they are the future. We, the older generations, need to take our rightful place as midwives to help them to birth their dreams; as shamans to lend an ear and a shoulder when they get weary; and as cheerleaders to cheer them on and celebrate their wins. But now more than ever we need to let their voices be heard, for they are the future that is trying break through to be born. We will all flourish when they are liberated to lead us into a brand new world.

Part 3
We The People

12
A brand new story

> To see a World in a Grain of Sand
> And a Heaven in a Wild Flower,
> Hold Infinity in the palm of your hand
> And Eternity in an hour.
> William Blake (1757–1827) "Auguries of Innocence"

Now, more than ever, we need to imagine our future, envision the world we want to create for our children, future generations, and for ourselves.[1] The tsunami of changes that has engulfed us at dizzying speed environmentally, technologically, economically, politically, and socially has shaken our sense of reality. These pervasive and unpredictable changes are causing deep profound global challenges in every area of our lives and are causing people to ask some crucial questions: What is important in life? What values do we need to embrace and build into our future? What kinds of organizations, institutions, communities, and lives do we want to create? People are struggling with these questions in all sectors of life. Moreover, there seems to be a growing desire to live with a sense of purpose, to be

---

[1] Versions of some passages in this chapter have appeared in Hunt, M. (2011, June 16). Compelling reasons for DreamMakers [Blog post]. http://michelehunt.blogspot.co.uk/2011/06/compelling-reasons-for-dreammakers.html; Hunt, M. *DreamMakers: Putting Vision and Values to Work*; and Hunt, M. (2011, August 12). And the Good News is, the World Has Ended, As We Know It [Blog post]. http://michelehunt.blogspot.co.uk/2011/08/and-good-news-is-world-has-ended-as-we.html.

deliberate about how we shape our lives, our organizations, institutions and communities. A whole new level of accountability and responsibility is required of all of us.

When I was growing up I thought that everything had already been discovered or invented. I used to marvel and wonder about what it must have been like to be a pioneer, a great inventor or a courageous explorer. Much to my surprise, I'm finding out, not by flying into space or trekking into the wilderness, or even inventing the next great gadget or app, rather by witnessing and participating in the world as it transforms into something it has never been before. A brand new world that has little or no resemblance to the old.

Although it looks and feels as if these changes came overnight, if we step back and reflect, they have been developing for a very long time. Like the fissures that form under the waterline of an iceberg, the cracks in our world have been multiplying and deepening for thousands of years. Globalism, exponential technological advancements, economic crises, environmental degradation, and shrinking resources have exposed the weak foundation on which many of our institutions, organizations, and even our communities were built. Our greatest error may be that we believed that the historical assumptions and beliefs on which we built our lives were sound, and strong enough to take us into the future. We were wrong. Many of our decisions and behaviors are based on false assumptions about people and nature. That weak foundation is now crumbling beneath the weight of our erroneous beliefs and our poor decisions. If we find the courage to honestly look at the world we have created, we cannot help but be moved to change and improve it. We disrespect and abuse the planet; the very place we depend on for life. We violate the most sacred law in most religious and moral teachings and ethical beliefs: "Thou Shall Not Kill." Women, half of the world's population, are often abused, very often oppressed and generally undervalued, resulting in the world being terribly and sadly out of balance. Contrary to what we expound, we put our children last; just look at the unconscionable number of children in our world that live in abject poverty, and that includes the richest countries in our world.

Most egregious, money has become the god so many of us worship. Most societies in our world have put money before people, families, communities, and our planet. We value quantity over quality and material things over humanity and life itself. Money in the United States has supplanted our democracy. Our political system is bought and sold like commodities, resulting in a powerful ruling class—the antithesis of democracy. This distortion is not compatible with democratic values and principles and it is not sustainable.

The most disturbing condition may be that we have lost our sense of community; our inextricable natural connection to one another. I believe the false assumption that we can live isolated and insulated from one another and from the planet that sustains us is the root of most of our problems today.

I heard a Native American mythology that tells the story about a time when the survivors of the great flood came together and made a plan to renew civilization. They decided to separate into four groups and set out in four different directions to discover and rebuild the world. The goal was for each group to bring their rich discoveries back for the benefit of the whole community. One group went east, another ventured west, one group went north, and the other south. The group that traveled north learned to become highly efficient, organized, analytical, and conservative—skills and perspectives they needed to navigate through their bitter cold environment and limited resources. Those who went east discovered the challenges of the dramatic topography, from the enormous mountain ranges to the vast deserts of the east. They learned to work in sync with the ominous topography that overshadowed them. The group that went west faced seemingly endless bodies of water. They learned courage, perseverance, and independence for they had to navigate through the unpredictable oceans with no assurance they would find land on the other side. The group that went south learned the art of celebration, dance and song for theirs was a world of vast resources, beauty and warmth. All of these discoveries, perspectives, and skills were gifts that could have benefited everyone when they reunited. But something went horribly wrong. As time went by, each group forgot that their mission was to explore their part of the world and to bring their beautiful discoveries and learnings back for the greater good of the whole community. Each group began to form their separate culture and norms. Soon their norms became their beliefs, and their beliefs became their truth. They began to judge the other groups, and soon their judgments turned into hate, and hate solidified their separation from one another. Eventually they began to venture out into the other groups' territories. They fought and killed one another for *their* version of the truth; each group believing *their* truth was *the* truth. The community mission was long forgotten and prejudice, hate, war and conflict became the way of life.

We have spent thousands of years learning to separate ourselves from one another and from the planet that sustains us. We are only now beginning to understand that we are deeply and inextricably connected, interdependent, and part of a greater whole. I am beginning to understand that the way out of my problems is the same way out of yours. I was talking with my dear friend Peter Senge and he made a statement that rings true: "start anywhere and you will end up everywhere." The internet and social media have helped us to see that everything and everyone is connected in some way. It has confirmed a quotation attributed to Albert Einstein:

> A human being is a part of a whole called by us the universe, a part limited in time and space. He experiences himself, his thoughts and feelings as something separated from the rest, a kind of optical delusion of his consciousness. This delusion is a kind of prison for us, restricting us to our personal desires and to affection for a few persons nearest to us. Our task must be to free ourselves from this prison by widening our circle of compassion to embrace all living creatures and the whole of nature in it beauty.

People are waking up! The most powerful catalyst for change lies within each of us. We all want clean water, clean air, good health, an education, a good job, and a sense of well-being. We also want to be heard, to participate, to contribute unique gifts, to be recognized, to be valued and most of all, to be loved. Whether we are business leaders, employees, consumers, families, or individuals, we want our lives to matter and we want to flourish and prosper.

People are extraordinary and capable of extraordinary things when we recognize our common bonds, aspirations, and our basic goodness. When we trust this truth, we have the capacity to collectively create the world we want. We don't have to wait for government or a leader or a hero or an extraordinary visionary to lead the way. The power that comes from our individual and collective vision, born out of our deeply held shared human values and our collective will to co-create a better world, is all that we need. So now is the most important time in the history of humankind for us to listen and learn from the different stories, different ways of thinking, and the different ways of organizing life, work, and communities. Then we can shed the past that no longer serves us and let the new world that wants to be born, to come through.

I often think of the caterpillar as it goes through its journey to become a butterfly. It serves as a useful metaphor for me during these times. Just before the caterpillar goes through its transformation, its cocoon is dark and rapidly deteriorating. Things must look very scary, messy, ugly and even life-threatening to that caterpillar. Soon, however, the caterpillar sees a vision of a better life and a butterfly emerges, but only when the caterpillar has learned to release itself from what it was, so it can become what it is meant to be next. When I walk through a field in the springtime I see some cocoons that have turned into coffins, but mostly I see beautiful, colorful, graceful butterflies enjoying the next stage of their lives.

We humans have the advantage of being able to *choose* our next stage of being in this world. We must choose well and wisely, and with great respect for the dignity of all of life. In this most remarkable time in the history of humankind, in spite of the tremendous challenges we face, we have within our reach, the means to make our hopes and dreams come true.

When I left Herman Miller to join President Clinton's administration, a group of employees gave me a beautiful gift that hangs on the wall in my office; I cherish it. It is a beautiful abstract painting by Carol Johnson of our planet with people connected at the head and the heart. The inscription below the painting is a poem called "Ascension"; it reads:

> Ascension fuels the passion to explore
> unchartered territories without hesitation or doubt:
> To be a change-maker while challenging
> others to make the same commitment;
> To provide a legacy by which others are
> motivated and transformed.

I believe that now is the most exciting time in the history of humankind to be alive. We have the opportunity and the responsibly to resist the urge to hold on to the past to enable us to co-recreate a brand new world. My dream is that we learn from the DreamMakers we read about to inspire us to discover and awaken the DreamMaker that is within each of us. When we put our collective hearts, minds, and imagination to work, we can co-create the lives, families, organizations, communities, and the world of our dreams. Like any great movement, the pursuit of a worldwide state where people and the planet can flourish together is an idea whose time has come.

About the author

Michele Hunt is a Transformation Catalyst and Strategic Advisor on leadership and organizational development and strategic communications. She helps leaders transform their cultures into vision-led, values-based, high-performance organizations. Michele is also a keynote speaker at conferences and meetings.

Michele was appointed by President Clinton as Director of the Federal Quality Institute, a bi-partisan initiative—Reinventing Government: Creating a Government that Works Better & Cost Less—led by Vice President Gore.

She previously served on the executive leadership team of Herman Miller, a Fortune 500 company, as Corporate Vice President For People, under the leadership of Max De Pree.

She served nine years with the Michigan Department of Corrections as the state's first female Deputy Warden of Programs for Rehabilitation in a male prison.

She serves on the advisory boards of the Fowler Center for Business as an Agent of World Benefit at the Weatherhead School of Management, Case Western Reserve University, the David L Cooperrider Center for Appreciative Inquiry at the Stiller School of Management, Champlain College, Images and Voices of Hope (IVOH), and the Detroit Windsor Dance Academy.

Michele is the author of *DreamMakers: Putting Vision and Values to Work*, with a Foreword by Max De Pree (2011), and *DreamMakers: Agents of Transformation* and she is a collaborator on the documentary, *DreamMakers*. She is a regular contributor to the *Huffington Post*.